D1371713

Penguin Education

Penguin Papers in Education

Language, the Learner and the School

Douglas Barnes is Lecturer in Education at the University of Leeds Institute of Education. He is editor of *Short Stories of Our Time* and author of *Drama in the Classroom* (A Dartmouth Seminar Paper).

James Britton is Professor of Education at Goldsmiths' College, University of London. He is editor of *Talking and Writing* (1967) and author of *Language and Learning* (Allen Lane The Penguin Press, 1970).

Harold Rosen is Lecturer in English at the University of London Institute of Education. He is author of 'The language of textbooks', in *Talking and Writing* and joint author, with James Britton and Nancy Martin, of the Schools Council publication, *Multiple Marking of English Compositions*.

Language, the Learner and the School

Revised edition

A Research Report by Douglas Barnes with a Contribution
by James Britton and a Discussion Document prepared
by Harold Rosen on behalf of the London Association
for the Teaching of English

Penguin Books

Penguin Books Ltd, Harmondsworth,
Middlesex, England
Penguin Books Inc., 7110 Ambassador Road,
Baltimore, Md 21207, U.S.A.
Penguin Books Australia Ltd, Ringwood,
Victoria, Australia

First published 1969
Reprinted 1969
Revised edition 1971
Reprinted 1971
Copyright © Douglas Barnes, James Britton, Harold Rosen
and the London Association for the Teaching of English,
1969, 1971

Made and printed in Great Britain by
Hazell Watson & Viney Ltd,
Aylesbury, Bucks
Set in Monotype Plantin

Contents

Part One

Language in the Secondary Classroom

A Study of Language Interaction in Twelve Lessons in the First Term of Secondary Education

Douglas Barnes

All the efforts of teachers in the Schools Council and elsewhere to develop new curricula may be abortive if curriculum development is taken to exclude examination of the part played by teachers in the curriculum, which is after all not a thing but an activity. It is too dangerous therefore to relegate the teacher's part to a subordinate and secondary topic called 'method'; how the teacher behaves must affect how and what the pupils learn. This paper is concerned with part of the teacher's behaviour, his language, and some of its effects upon his pupils. It does not claim to be a formal research report, but is intended to be of direct use to teachers in their work.

Defining the Task

Books whose titles include the words 'language' and 'education' usually concern themselves with examining the terms in which education is discussed. An exception to this is F. D. Flower's *Language and Education* which applies the insights of contemporary linguistic studies to the teaching of the mother tongue. There is, however, a third area where language and educational studies overlap, and this is the study of the language of the classroom. Not only is the teacher–class group a social microcosm, but one which also interacts with the social macrocosm of which it is a part. And as the complicated commerce within the group is largely carried on through language, so is it largely through language that society explicitly or covertly defines and limits the activities of the group. Thus, to study the language of the classroom is to study both the learning processes and some of the internal and external constraints upon it.

My attention was first directed to this area of inquiry by Harold Rosen of the University of London Institute of Education. In an unpublished paper entitled 'The Problems of Impersonal Language' he writes:

But the verbalization of concepts within different subjects has a complex history; it is probably not a simple matter of perfectly evolved language which embodies one kind of rational thought. The models we look at are social institutions, and the differences between say the language of geology and the language of history may be in part due to the different history of these two subjects. In all events we should set about distinguishing between the linguistic-conventional and the linguistic-intellectual, so that we can understand that traditional formulations are not sacrosanct.

Having thus questioned the functions of subject-specific linguistic registers, Mr Rosen in a later passage looks at some of their implications for learning.

Much of the language encountered in school looks at pupils across a chasm. Some fluent children . . . adopt the jargon and parrot whole stretches of lingo. Personal intellectual struggle is made irrelevant and the personal view never asked for. Language and experience are torn asunder. Worse still, many children find impersonal language mere noise. It is alien in its posture, conventions, and strategies. . . . These are extremes. Many children have areas of confidence and understanding but frequently have to resort to desperate mimicry to see them through.

Mr Rosen had also suggested in conversation that there is a 'language of secondary education' not specific to curricular subjects, but forming an even greater potential barrier to learning. It was with questions and surmises such as these that I first approached the study of language in the secondary school classroom.

There is a considerable American literature concerned with the analysis of classroom interaction, much of it stemming from the work of Ned A. Flanders. Most of the studies, however, restrict themselves to statements about whole lessons, and do not examine the details of the ebb and flow of activity during the parts of the lesson. Quotations of the actual words used are hardly to be found; writers tend to use made-up exchanges to illustrate their meaning. The desire to make general and quantifiable statements has directed the attention of most investigators away from the considerations raised in this paper. (John Holt is a notable exception.) Flanders does however distinguish two categories of 'student talk' – that in response to the teacher and what he too describes as 'student-initiated'.

A number of pieces of work have been done upon the linguistic register used by scientists, for example, by C. L. Barber. What Dr Barber calls 'stylistic variations' seem to be part of Mr Rosen's 'language of secondary education', which suggests that this name (used throughout this paper) would be too limiting in other contexts.

My original conception was of a 'Study of the linguistic expectations set up in first-year lessons in secondary schools'. I expected that generalizations drawn from a few secondary lessons could be put beside others drawn from primary schools, and light thrown on some difficulties of adjustment faced by new entries to secondary schools. I was able to attempt the first part of this when, in October 1966, I undertook a series of seminars in 'Language and Education' with teachers studying for a Diploma in Curricular Studies at the University of Leeds Institute of Education. As they were also attending my lectures on this subject I determined that the seminars should be devoted to practical study; they tape-recorded first-year lessons taught by friends, transcribed them, and analysed them according to a scheme I supplied. The teachers participating found this an enlightening and disturbing task. The study provided information on far more matters than I had expected, and did so in a way which challenged the group to inspect their own assumptions about teaching. It undoubtedly provided an excellent method for the study of teaching. The results were not, however, of a kind to encourage me to move on to the language of the primary school.

This led to a redefinition of the task. I now saw it as a

preliminary investigation of the interaction between the linguistic expectations (drawn from home and primary school experience) brought by pupils to their secondary schools, and the linguistic demands set up (implicitly or explicitly) by the teachers in the classrooms. It seemed likely that extraneous barriers were introduced into children's learning (a) by linguistic forms whose function was social rather than intrinsic to the material and processes being learnt, and (b) by unfamiliar socio-linguistic demands and constraints arising in the control systems of the secondary classroom. It was in terms such as these that I embarked on the descriptive study of lessons experienced by eleven-year-old children during their first half-term in a secondary school.

Obtaining Material

Our purpose was to record the whole language environment of the children during lesson-time. We were interested in both spoken and written language, and in the child as producer and receiver. We expected our sources to include:

Spoken language
(a) The teacher's oral exposition.
(b) The teacher's questions, and the resulting teacher-initiated exchanges.
(c) Discussion – i.e. partly pupil-initiated.
(d) Language used in the course of the teacher–pupil relationship – e.g. persuasion, criticism, relationship-establishing.
(e) Pupil to pupil language.

Written language
(a) Textbooks used during the lesson.
(b) Teachers' notes – duplicated, dictated, or copied from the blackboard.
(c) Writing – teacher-defined   (i) in form.
                                    (ii) in content.
(d) Writing – wholly or partly pupil-defined.

(e) Other written material – e.g. charts.

The investigators obtained permission to go into lessons with a tape-recorder, recorded the lessons, and supplemented the recording with notes of:

(a) The children's contributions, which were often incomprehensible on tape.
(b) Significant actions and gestures accompanying speech.
(c) Writing and diagrams from the blackboard.
(d) Sketches of any apparatus in use.
(e) The proportion of pupils who spoke during the lesson. (This last has proved almost impossible to perform.)

They also borrowed textbooks and selected exercise books in order to make photocopies of relevant passages.

In 1966 the teachers collaborating with me made separate arrangements to record lessons being taught by teachers whom they knew well. In 1967 I arranged with the headmaster of a comprehensive school to follow a first-year class through a whole day of lessons. (The implications of this are discussed later.) On both occasions the pupils were in about the sixth week of attendance at that secondary school, with the exception of two mathematics lessons in 1966. In 1967 there were two investigators present in each lesson: in both years the tape-recording was transcribed by an investigator who had been present during the lesson (with the exception of Lesson G). The lessons can be tabulated:

1966

	Secondary modern (mixed)	Comprehensive (mixed)	Grammar (boys)	Grammar (girls)
Maths (2 lessons)	Lesson B (man)		Lesson A* (man)	
Science (3 lessons)		Lesson G (physics) (man)	Lesson F (chemistry) (man)	
		Lesson E (biology) (woman)		

*The investigator recorded a second-year class in error.

1966

	Secondary modern (mixed)	Comprehensive (mixed)	Grammar (boys)	Grammar (girls)
Geography/ history (2 lessons)				Lesson C (history) (woman) Lesson D (geography) (woman)
Total	1	2	2	2

Seven lessons were recorded and transcribed, though one was with an older class.

1967

The class chosen was the fourth out of seven first-year streamed classes in a mixed comprehensive school in an industrial area.

During the day seven lessons were recorded, but two (French and drama) have not been transcribed or analysed. The five that remain – which constitute the main body of material – are:

Lesson J   Mathematics (woman)
Lesson K   History (man)
Lesson L   Physics (woman)
Lesson M   English (man)
Lesson N   Religious Education (man)

The Analysis of the Material

The purpose of this initial study was to find what consistencies could be perceived which would link patterns in the teacher's linguistic behaviour to patterns in the children's learning. Thus the analytical instrument inevitably called for interpretation of the material. The instrument has been several times revised during the work; in its latest form the method of analysis is organized as follows:

(a) Teacher's questions

Analyse *all* questions asked by the teacher into these categories:

   1. *Factual* ('What?' questions)
    (i) naming
   (ii) information
   2. *Reasoning* ('How?' and 'Why?' questions)
    (i) 'closed' reasoning – recalled sequences
    (ii) 'closed' reasoning – not recalled
   (iii) 'open' reasoning
   (iv) observation
   3. *'Open' questions not calling for reasoning*
   4. *Social*
    (i) control ('Won't you ... ?' questions)
    (ii) appeal ('Aren't we ... ?' questions)
   (iii) other

Notes on questions

Naming questions ask pupils to give a name to some phenomenon without requiring them to show insight into its use.

Reasoning questions require pupils to 'think aloud' – to construct, or reconstruct from memory, a logically organized sequence.

Recall questions are concerned with summoning up required knowledge from memory.

Closed questions have only one acceptable answer; whereas to

Open questions a number of different answers would be acceptable. Open questions might be factual in some circumstances: for example, a request for 'any fraction', where the range of choices open to the pupil is unusually wide. (It is necessary to check apparently open questions by examining the teacher's reception of pupils' replies, which may show that he will accept only one reply to a question framed in apparently open terms. Such questions might be called 'pseudo-questions'.)

Observation questions are intended to include those questions (about phenomena immediately present to the children) which require them to interpret what they perceive. (There may be difficulty in distinguishing some of these from 'naming questions'.)

Control questions are directed towards imposing the teacher's wishes upon the class.

Appeal questions, which ask pupils to agree, or share an attitude, or remember an experience, are less directive than control questions: that is, it is possible for children to reject them without necessarily giving offence.

(b) Pupils' participation

1. Was all speech initiated by the teacher? Note any exchanges initiated by pupils.

(i) If these were initiated by questions, were they 'What?', 'How?' or 'Why?' questions? Were they directed towards the material studied or towards performing the given tasks?

(ii) If they were unsolicited statements or comments, how did the teacher deal with them?

2. Were pupils required to express personal responses
  (i) of perception?
  (ii) of feeling and attitude?

3. How large a part did pupils take in the lesson? Were any silent throughout? How large a proportion took a continuous part in discussion?

4. What did pupils' contributions show of their success in following the lesson?

5. How did the teacher deal with inappropriate contributions?

(c) The language of instruction

1. Did the teacher use a linguistic register specific to his subject? Find examples of vocabulary and structures characteristic of the register.

2. Did any pupils attempt to use this register? Was it expected of them?

3. What did the teacher do to mediate between the language and experience of his pupils and the language and concepts of the subject?

4. Did the teacher use forms of language which, though not specific to his subject, might be outside the range of eleven-year-olds? Find examples, if any.

(d) Social relationships

1. How did the relationship between teacher and pupils show itself in language?

2. Were there differences between the language of instruction and the language of relationships? Was the language of relationships intimate or formal? Did it vary during the lesson?

(e) Language and other media

1. Was language used for any tasks that might have been done better by other means (e.g. pictures, practical tasks, demonstrations)?

2. Were pupils expected to verbalize any non-verbal tasks they engaged in?

Limitations

(a) The sample – even if all twelve lessons are included – is far too small to allow for any statements more positive than hypotheses. Any conclusions must be methodological, or indications for further investigation, or concerned with the appropriateness of such study to the training of teachers, or limited to statements about these lessons and no others.

(b) Most of the teachers in the 1966 sample are mature, confident, and on friendly terms with the one investigator present: there seems no reason to think that the investigation caused any major change in their teaching behaviour. On the other hand, the sample was so diverse as to discourage even the most qualified generalization.

(c) In 1967 the choice of a single class required that the invitation be given to a headmaster, and not to individual teachers. This meant that the teachers whose lessons were investigated were not necessarily very eager to collaborate. In the event, they tended to be young and more disturbed by our presence than were the 1966 teachers. Some were clearly nervous, and even unwilling. Others seemed to have 'over-prepared' the material they were teaching.

(d) Since adults intuitively adjust their language forms

to different audiences, our presence – and that of our tape-recorders – probably caused some non-deliberate changes in language.

(e) The teachers had been told that the investigators were interested in the language used in the lessons. Although they were asked to carry on with normal work, some may have slanted their lesson more towards spoken language than would otherwise have been the case.

Interrelation of Results

As the analytical instrument indicates, the demands made upon the pupils were examined under five heads:

Questions asked by the teacher
The participation demanded of (or allowed to) the pupils
The language used in instruction
The language used in social control
Relationship of language to other activities and media

Clearly these are matters of analytic convenience, and not separate categories. The teachers' questions, for example, are drawn from the language of social control and from the language of instruction, having been extracted for more quantitative analysis. The questions about pupil participation require more than description of language: the material is here used to make qualitative judgements about teaching and learning. Something similar is true of the relationship of language to other activities and media. These are not, however, five separate issues; in pursuing them one has the impression of making five different approaches to the same complex of social behaviour. To change one might be to change all.

It will be seen from pp. 16–17 that we sorted teachers' questions into four categories: factual, reasoning, open questions not calling for reasoning, and social. We also distinguished which of the factual and reasoning questions were open-ended and which closed-ended. When we discussed particular questions which occurred in the lessons we had recorded, we did not always find it easy to assign questions to a particular category, but we all found that this discussion of particular questions threw light on our teaching.

The table below shows my own analysis of all the questions asked during the five lessons recorded in 1967. It has so far proved extremely difficult to define the categories in such a way that the analysis can be reproduced by another investigator; nevertheless this seems a potentially useful starting point.

Tables of Teachers' Questions in Five Lessons

Lesson	*J* Maths	*L* Science	*K* History	*M* English	*N* R.E.
(a) Analysis of questions					
Factual (Category 1)	36	9	30	19	21
Reasoning (Category 2)	17	19	4	6	7
Open questions not calling for reasoning (Category 3)	0	0	0	0	0
Social (Category 4)	19	5	5	12	9
Total number of questions	72	33	39	37	37
(b) Open questions					
Number of open questions (Factual and Reasoning)	9	9	8	12	1
Open questions as % of total	17	32	23·5	48	3·6

Figures of this kind can be taken to represent the teachers' covert interpretation of the nature of what they were teaching – that is, the interpretation *that they were acting upon* whatever they may have told themselves about the purpose of the lesson. And this covert version of their subject is important because it will be 'learnt' by the pupils *as part of the role of being a learner in that subject*.

What most impressed us in these figures was the predominance of factual over reasoning questions in the three arts subjects lessons, that is, seventy factual questions against seventeen reasoning questions. Typical factual questions were: 'Does anyone know any of the books or poems Homer wrote?' 'Where do you think they kept the lamps?' (The answer had been given in a previous lesson.) 'We call it AABBA ... and what do we call that?' (The answer finally given by the teacher was 'Rhyming scheme'.) Reasoning questions included: 'Now what makes a language beautiful?' 'Why do you think they used bread for spoons?' 'That second line's not right. [Refers to metrical pattern.] Why not?' This proportion suggests that the three arts teachers were teaching as though their tasks were more concerned with information than thought. If so, this is the version of the subjects that the children were learning. The teachers would perhaps be surprised to discover this about their teaching and might wish to change it. (Or they might believe that this is a proper proportion between information and thought, in which case it would be difficult to agree with them.) This analysis goes some way towards enabling a teacher to find out about aspects of his teaching of which he may normally be unaware.

Almost equally surprising is the predominance of factual over reasoning questions in the mathematics lesson. This is explained by our decision to categorize as factual questions (a) those which required pupils to count items in a diagram ('How many squares?'), and (b) the kind that, for example, required pupils to know that if a whole is divided into six parts each part is called a sixth (i.e. a naming question, Category 1(i)). The high proportion of reasoning questions in the science lesson well represents the pattern of the lesson: the teacher made several demonstrations to the class and required them to explain to her what was happening, asking for example: 'Why did it go off just at that point?'

Entirely 'open' questions hardly ever occur, so in distinguishing closed from open questions we were in fact distinguishing those cases in which the teacher will accept only a single answer expressed in a relatively predetermined form from those cases in which he will accept either a wide (but not infinite) range of answers, or a small limited range but in any order. Some of the most difficult distinctions arise when the teacher clearly knows the kind of answer he wants so that the decision to categorize as open or closed rests upon a subjective assessment of the extent to which he wishes his pupils to explore the alternative formulations, relationships and contexts of this reply. Thus this part of the analysis requires an interpretation of the teacher's behaviour which cannot be made entirely objective while the evidence is often ambiguous.

Examples of extremely open questions are: 'Tell me any fraction', and 'What books have you been reading?' When a teacher asked, 'How do we recognize what a limerick is?' he was ready to accept four answers in any order, but it was clear that he knew in advance exactly what these were. Questions of this kind were categorized as 'open', though with some hesitation. Another borderline case was: 'Why did it [a flame] go down?' in answer to which the teacher accepted, 'The gas wasn't coming for it to be burnt', and added, 'There wasn't as much gas spare.' She knew what answer she wanted, but was also willing to accept the pupil's formulation, so – again with hesitation – we categorized this as 'open'.

Although the proportions (given in the table) of open questions to the total number of open and closed questions may not be entirely reliable, their tendency is clear enough. In spite of our perhaps over-generous allocation of doubtful cases to the 'open' category, the proportion is low in all lessons except English. (The open questions in the English lesson were largely ones requiring the pupils to find likenesses between two poems; the teacher accepted a wide range of replies relating either to form or to meaning.) These proportions can be taken to mean that four of the teachers were taking their task to be more a matter of handing over ready-made material, whether facts or processes, than a matter of encouraging pupils to participate actively and to bring their own thoughts and recollections into the conversation. (Very few questions indeed were asked because the teacher was truly ignorant of the answer and wanted to know; the implications of this for conversation bear pondering.)

If an analysis such as this were applied to a larger representative sample of first-year lessons and gave similar results to those tabulated above, it would be reasonable for those responsible for curricular planning to ask themselves (i) whether arts subjects *should* at this level be predominantly factual, and (ii) whether more open-ended learning in arts and sciences *might be more effective*. This might lead to questioning whether they wished to encourage pupils in habits of acceptance or habits of improvization.

Both the 1966 and 1967 lessons provided many examples of what the investigators came to call 'pseudo-questions', since they appeared open but were treated by the teacher as closed. For example, in Lesson L (the 1967 science lesson) the teacher asked:

T   What can you tell me about a bunsen burner, Alan?
P.1   A luminous and non-luminous flame.
T   A luminous and non-luminous flame. . . . When do you have a luminous flame?
P.1   When there's . . . there's oxygen.
T   When the airhole is closed. . . . When is it a non-luminous flame, Gary?
P.2   When . . . when the air-hole is open.
T   Right . . . good . . .

The original question requires the pupil to abstract from all possible statements about the bunsen burner, that one which the teacher's unstated criterion finds acceptable. He is presumably helped to do this by memor-

ies of a former lesson on the topic. Our samples suggest
that it is not unusual for teachers to ask children to conform to an unstated criterion; children might participate
better if the criteria were explicit.

Another group of 'pseudo-questions' appears to relate
to classroom procedure but should perhaps be reckoned as
'social' in function. For example, Lesson F (1966; grammar school; chemistry lesson) has several such questions:

T   Now what we want is a method whereby we can take off
      this . . . um . . . green material . . . this green stuff off the
      grass and perhaps one two of you can suggest how we
      might do this. . . . Yes?
P.1   Boil it.
T   Boil it? What with?
P.1   Some water in a beaker and . . .
T   Yes, there's that method . . . we could do it and . . . um . . .
      I think probably you could guess how we might be able
      to do it by what we've already got out in the laboratory.
      How do you think we might do it?
      [Pestle and mortar are on bench.]
P.2   Could pound it . . .
T   Pound it up with water . . . and that's exactly what we're
      going to do.

The teacher having, perhaps necessarily, predetermined the method to be used, asks the question in order
to involve his pupils more personally in the activity. But
this forces him (a) to interrupt a pupil who is thinking
aloud ('some water in a beaker and . . .') and (b) to reject
that pupil's reasonable suggestion. It could be argued that
both of these are to be avoided for pedagogical reasons.

In the 1967 lessons there was not one example of an
'open question not calling for reasoning'. This would
match teachers' impressions that those children who come
up from primary schools ready to explore personal experience aloud and to offer anecdotal contributions to
discussion cease to do so within a few weeks of arrival.
Clearly they learn in certain lessons that anecdotes are
held by the teacher to be irrelevant. It can be hypothesized that they begin to take part in each new 'subject' by

taking in their teacher's behaviour as a reciprocal element in their own role as learners, so that his voice becomes one 'voice' in their own internal dialogues. Thus, because the teacher never asks questions that can be answered by anecdotes, anecdotes cease to be a part of their own thinking about the subject, and become 'unthinkable' as contributions to class discussion.

If this hypothetical interpretation is valid, the matter is of considerable interest to teachers, such as English specialists, who take it as part of their task to help children to develop their power of using language to deal with the realm of private and personal meaning. Some children seem to generalize the irrelevance of 'personal' statement, for example, into writing tasks where the exploration of personal meaning would not be out of place.

Pupil Participation

It is not easy to measure pupil participation, especially since it is the quality of participation which matters, rather than its vociferousness. Perhaps the main point can be made impressionistically: both of the teams of investigators, in 1966 and 1967, all of them experienced teachers, when asked what their sharpest impression of the materials had been, first mentioned 'passivity'. This is in spite of several very successful question-and-answer lessons, and two 1967 lessons in improvised drama and oral French (which have not been included in the material). Teachers talk far more than pupils can reply; and the reply time is shared amongst thirty or more pupils. Even if it were shared equally between them, none would have taken a large part in the day's *overt* activity. But this is no more than an impression; it would not be impossible to believe that children were participating vividly but in silence. (Most passages quoted in this paper are chosen precisely because they show teacher–pupil interaction, so they may give the impression of more interaction than appears when the lesson is seen as a whole.)

One of the most interesting questions raised by the material relates to the ways in which the teacher covertly signals to his pupils what their role as learners is to be. This has partly appeared above in the analysis of teachers' questions: in the 1967 sample, pupils are normally expected to reproduce information or reasoning, rather than to think for themselves. The 1966 lessons were not dissimilar. This question is reverted to in more detail in the subsections headed 'Thinking aloud' and 'Pupil-initiated sequences', but it is implicit throughout this section.

This section is subdivided into:

(a) The gulf between teacher and taught
(b) Thinking aloud
(c) Questioning to a predetermined end
(d) The teacher supplies a structure
(e) The demand for explicitness
(f) Pupil-initiated sequences

(a) The gulf between teacher and taught

Since most questions in the sample were closed-ended, pupils were seldom invited to think aloud, to generate new sequences of thought, to explore implications. (One example of a teacher's cutting short such verbal improvisation in the interests of his preconceived plan has already been quoted.) Some educationists (e.g. J. S. Bruner, *On Knowing*) have held that such productive activities add greatly to learning. If the lessons of the sample are typical in this respect, teachers might well question their own attitudes and behaviour in the classroom. Are they teaching their younger pupils that to learn is to accept factual material passively and reproduce it for matching against the teacher's model, to be judged right or wrong? Should they reconsider their use of full class or small group discussion? These questions are pedagogical. What a study such as this can hope to contribute to answering them is further understanding of the implications of different kinds of classroom 'discussion', since the word has different meanings for different teachers. The teacher in Lesson F (1966; chemistry; grammar school) might have described the following as 'discussion'. He was explaining that milk is an example of the suspension of solids in a liquid:

T   You get the white ... what we call casein ... that's ... er ... protein ... which is good for you ... it'll help to build bones ... and the white is mainly the casein and so it's not actually a solution ... it's a suspension of very fine particles together with water and various other things which are dissolved in water ...

P.1 Sir, at my old school I shook my bottle of milk up and when I looked at it again all the side was covered with ... er ... like particles and ... er ... could they be the white particles in the milk. .. ?

P.2 Yes, and gradually they would sediment out, wouldn't they, to the bottom. .. ?

P.3 When milk goes very sour though it smells like cheese, doesn't it?

P.4 Well, it is cheese, isn't it, if you leave it long enough?

T   Anyway can we get on? ... We'll leave a few questions for later.

What is happening here? The teacher talks about milk, using his specialist language to help him perceive it as an exemplar of the category 'suspension', and to free him from all other contexts and categories it might appear in. But for his pupils 'milk' collocates not with 'suspension' but with 'cheese', 'school', 'shook', 'bottle'; they perceive it in that context and his use of 'casein' and 'fine particles' signals to only two of them that some different response is expected. Pupil 1 recognizes 'particles' and, searching his experience, comes up with lumps of curd. Trying to conform to the teacher's expectation, he manages 'the side was covered with ... like particles', his uncertainty finding its expression in the deprecatory 'like'. Pupil 2 follows this line of thought and, associating the idea of sedimentation with suspended particles, tries 'they would sediment out'. These two pupils are beginning to use the language of science to make the specifically scientific abstraction from the experience. But Pupils 3 and 4, although they are *attentive to what the teacher appears to be saying*, are unable to make this abstraction; the words the teacher has used do not signal to them which aspects of the 'milk' experience should be abstracted. Far from helping them to bridge the gulf between his frame of reference and theirs, the teacher's language acts as a barrier, of which he seems quite unaware. They are left with their own first-hand experience – 'it smells like cheese'. The state of the other less articulate members of the class can only be guessed at. The teacher, frightened by his sudden glimpse of the gulf between them, hastily continues with the lesson he has planned.

The teacher teaches within his frame of reference; the pupils learn in theirs, taking in his words, which 'mean' something different to them, and struggling to incorporate this meaning into their own frames of reference. The language which is an essential instrument to him is a barrier to them. How can the teacher help his pupils to use this language as he does? Certainly not by turning away from the problem.

Besides this we may place a sequence from Lesson K (1967; history) in which the teacher, aware of the gulf between what the word 'language' means to him and to his pupils, attempts to bridge it.

T   Now what do we mean by language?
P.1 The alphabet.
T   That's part of it . . . what else?
P.2 How to speak.
T   How to speak . . . yes . . . what else? . . . What else do you do with a language apart from speaking it?
P.3 Pronounce it.
T   Well that's part of speaking. . . . What else?
P.4 Learn to say it.
T   Still the same thing . . . yes?
P   Sir, you can tell the countries by the language they speak.
T   Yes, but what else can we use a language for? We don't always speak a language. . . . I don't always speak a

language when I want to get something over to someone
who is not in the same room . . . probably a long way
away . . . I can't shout or use the telephone. . . . What do
I do?

P   Write.

T   I write . . . right, therefore it's the written word as well as
the spoken word.

Without the initial question the teacher is unlikely to
have known how hard the pupils found it to conceive of
language as a whole. He pursued the matter with some
determination, but even at the end one does not know how
far his references to the 'written word' and the 'spoken
word' could mean anything to his pupils. He has, however, enabled a few pupils to take an active part in testing
how far their meanings match with his.

Information about the 'gulf' can only come when the
teacher either asks an open question (such as 'What do we
mean by language?') or when he requires pupils to use
what they have been taught, as in writing. The disadvantage of writing as a means of making knowledge
their own is that the reply to it may be both delayed and
restricted to a general comment or assessment. It is in the
give and take of reciprocal discussion that the pupil can
best try out the new concepts and modify them in response to the teacher's replies.

(b) Thinking aloud

At times teachers do try to involve pupils in exploring the
subject

(i) by requiring a pupil to 'think aloud', to generate a
sequence of ideas for himself;

(ii) by discussion in which the teacher by questioning
leads his pupils to a preconceived end;

(iii) by providing a linguistic structure for a pupil to
complete.

These three will be the subject of this section and the
following two. Examples of these categories are *very*

infrequent and tend to involve only one child. For example, it is not easy in the twelve lessons to find occasions
when pupils are required to think aloud. One occurs in
Lesson G (1966; physics; comprehensive school). The
teacher had put in front of the class a mechanism illus-
trating the working of an aneroid barometer. After a
lengthy demonstration with explanations, the teacher
asked about the function of part of the apparatus. A
pupil replied:

Well the silver knob is to turn that pointer. . . . If you turn
that to say say twenty or whatever the other hand says . . . when
the other hand moves you can see the difference in pressure.

This clearly illustrates some of the linguistic–conceptual
apparatus that the pupil lacks, and which he will need if
he is ever to be complete master of the process. He lacks a
general term such as 'the position of' for the phrase
'say twenty or whatever the other hand says'. More
important, he needs to be able to name an intermediate
conceptual stage between setting the pointer and reading
off the difference in pressure. This would produce something like: 'from *the angle between* the two pointers, you
can see . . .'. Nor has the pupil realized that 'when the
hand moves' does not make the time scale explicit
enough, though he seems to understand what he means.
These kinds of mental and verbal inadequacy cannot
easily be dealt with by direct instruction because they are
so difficult to predict. It is only in relatively 'open'
discussion that they become apparent. (Unfortunately a
gap in the recording prevented us from studying how the
teacher dealt with this.)

The physics lesson quoted above contained a number of
similar examples, but these are infrequent in all other
lessons in both years. This is partly related to the lack of
open-ended questions, but questions which required
pupils to reason about given material were also infrequent.
The lack of open-ended questions may – it could be
argued – arise from these young pupils' ignorance of the

topic, which would delay their active participation to such time as they have an enabling knowledge. But this would not explain the lack of more limited questions, based upon given material, and requiring pupils at a simple level to operate the intellectual processes of the subject. This certainly happened in some mathematics lessons, but in general the pupils appeared to be 'learning' that learning is a passive receptive process. This may well make some of them unsatisfactory pupils at a later stage when more active participation is required of them.

In Lesson L (1967; physics) the pupils were asked to watch the behaviour of flames in a tin can into which gas was piped. (This was the lesson with 32 per cent open questions: the following is perhaps the most successful of the questions requiring interpretation of the teacher's demonstration.)

T   Now when I turn the gas tap on . . . what's coming out of the top?

P   Flames . . . luminous flames.

T   What's coming out of the top of the tin?

P   Um . . . air . . . that's been burnt . . . gas that's been burnt.

T   Good. It's burnt gas . . . spare gas . . . so what's that tell you about the inside of the tin? . . . what is there inside there?

P   Gas.

T   It's full of gas, right. . . . Now then, I'm going to turn off the gas and I want you to watch carefully . . . watch the flame and see anything . . . any change that you can . . . and also watch the tin carefully. . . . Right, I shall turn it off. What did you see as soon as I turned it off?

P   The flame went down.

T   Why did it go down?

P   Cos the . . . it wasn't . . . the gas wasn't coming for it to be burnt.

T   There wasn't as much gas spare . . . we've burnt off the spare gas.

Here the teacher has succeeded in limiting the task so that it is quite explicit: the pupils do not have to guess at the criteria which she is using in judging the relevance of an answer. Yet the questions are relatively open ended; they do little to constrict the language in which the child might answer (contrast for example the passage from Lesson F about milk); they encourage the children to improvise explanations within the given frame of reference. It is worth noting that this teacher made it possible for pupils to pause and reshape their utterances: 'Cos the . . . it wasn't . . . the gas wasn't . . .'.

In Lesson N (1967; religious education) an exchange occurred which can be contrasted with this. The teacher was asking for the recall of information about life in New Testament Palestine.

T   How did they get the water from the well? . . . Do you remember? . . . Yes?

P.1 They . . . ran the bucket down . . . er . . . and it was fastened on to this bit of string and it . . . [here the words become inaudible for a phrase or two] . . . other end to the water.

T   You might do it that way. . . . Where did they put the water . . . John?

P.2 In a big . . . er . . . pitcher.

T   Good . . . in a pitcher . . . which they carried on their . . . ?

P   Heads.

The question 'How did they get the water from the well?' has signalled to Pupil 1 that this is a relatively open question to which an improvised sequence would be appropriate. His reply, the quality of which is here irrelevant, is met by 'You might do it that way' spoken with an intonation expressing doubt. That is, Pupil 1's answer is rejected, though in a polite form of words. Pupil 2 suggests an answer *of a different kind*; he intuits – or remembers – that his teacher does not want improvised reasoning but the name of an object. His reply 'In a big . . . er . . . pitcher' is accepted and carried further with a promptness which signals *to both pupils* that this is what was required in the first place. It might be surmised that these pupils are not only learning about Palestine but also about the kinds of reciprocal behaviour appropriate to a teacher–pupil relationship, that is, learning when not to think. (It should be remembered that they are in their sixth week in a new school.)

This is an example of the kind of question which the investigators have come to call a 'pseudo-question', in that while it has the form of an open question the teacher's treatment of replies shows that he is willing to accept only one answer.

(c) Questioning to a preconceived end

Teachers who try to deal directly with sequences of thought may involve themselves in other problems. In Lesson E (1966; biology; comprehensive school) the teacher was recapitulating material previously taught:

T   How does the fish obtain the oxygen from the water? What happens. . . ? Stephen?

P   It allows the water to run over its gills and the . . . er . . . and extracts the oxygen.

T   First of all think of it in stages, Stephen. Where does the water go first of all?

P   Miss, it enters the mouth and then it passes over the gills taking out the oxygen. Then it comes out of the gills.

T   Comes out of the back of the gill-cover. . . .

The difficulty for the pupil seems to arise not only from the nature of the subject-matter. If he were explaining this to an equal for a given purpose, his choice of items would be determined by that purpose and the extent of his knowledge. But he is explaining this to a teacher who already knows it, and for an unstated purpose, so he can only construct a criterion for choosing items by projecting himself into the teacher's mind, partly in response to her signals of acceptance or rejection. The teacher seems to be demanding more specific references; the problem for the pupil must be to determine what will be relevant and acceptable – by what criteria the teacher is judging relevance. Once he has made these (usually unspoken) criteria his own he will be able to join in the teacher's mode of thought. Why, for example, should he specify 'the back of the gill-cover' since he has not specified 'the front of the mouth'? (It is worth noting how the pupil has searched for 'extracts the oxygen' after an abortive start 'and the ...' on a different formulation. He has already internalized some of his teacher's criteria.)

A carefully guided argument can be valuable when the pupil is on the point of comprehending the teacher's criterion, and can lead to the sudden jump of insight needed. In Lesson M (1967; English) the teacher is aiming to sharpen his pupils' awareness of traditional verse-scansion; a pupil has read aloud a limerick she has written.

T   'Then to his surprise' ... yes?
P   'He slowly began to rise'.
T   'He slowly began to rise'. .... We've got too many haven't we? Di dee didi dee. .... Then we could really do with 'He ...' ?
P   'He began to rise'.
T   'He began to rise' ... but it's not very good, is it? There's too many in it. .... You've got to ...
P   'He *start*ed to rise'.
T   'He started to rise' ... that's better ...

The pupil's heavy emphasis on the first syllable of 'started' shows that she has taken in the teacher's criterion. (One wonders what would have happened if she had been asked to make her discovery explicit.) Sequences resulting in a flash of insight are infrequent. This is the only un-doubted case in the material.

In the 1967 mathematics lesson (J) the proportion of reasoning questions to factual questions was 17:36, yet of these only nine were categorized as 'open'. The teacher was giving very closely defined reasoning tasks and on the whole requiring pupils to take only one step at a time.

This has been true of the two 1966 mathematics lessons also, and all three show this to be an efficient teaching method whenever the teacher is able to formulate in ad-vance the process to be taught.

The next example shows that even in mathematics this may at times narrow the teacher's perception of the teaching possibilities. The teacher in Lesson J was requiring her pupils to operate the concepts of fractions by dividing rectangles into parts. She had prepared a large diagram to illustrate $\frac{3}{6} = \frac{1}{2}$:

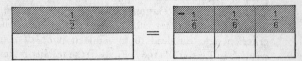

She put this on show – though many of the pupils could apparently not see the diagram – and told the class to divide a half into sixths. After a pause she picked up one boy's work:

T   Why aren't I very happy with that one? . . . I can't get cross and say it's wrong but I'm not happy . . . [pause] Come on . . . think of what I asked you to do . . . Linda?

P.1   You told us not to shade the second one but put in the number of sixths.

T   Oh no nothing like that. . . . You had to shade in the same area as a half. . . . Well, has he shaded in the same area?

Ps   [replies are inaudible]

T   What's his shape . . . what's his shape? . . . What's it like?

P.2   He's just put two on the top and one on the bottom.

T   Right . . . well, it's like a fat L or something he's drawn. . . . It's right, isn't it Shaw?

P.3   Yes Miss.

T   No, so it doesn't illustrate our point.

It did however show that some pupils – the boy whose diagram was being discussed, and Pupil 1, Linda – had

not understood what they were doing. In this sequence
the teacher does not make explicit either what the task is,
or how it is that the boy's diagram 'doesn't illustrate our
point'. Moreover, this might have seemed a useful
opportunity to demonstrate that:

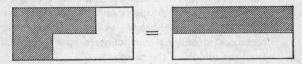

This possibility seems to have been concealed from her by
the admirable thoroughness of her prepared plan.

An enormous amount of talk washes over pupils in
lessons. Their problem must be to select from it those
utterances which make explicit the criteria by which their
performances will be judged. Some teachers mark these
utterances with different intonation patterns and vocal
quality. When teachers do not do this, pupils must be
faced with a difficult problem of selective attentiveness.
It seems that some children so largely fail to perceive the
nature of the given tasks that they are in effect not solving
problems but copying external models; Linda may be one
of these children, and so may a child (not quoted above)
whose attention seemed to be directed to the colour of
the shading. On the other hand, the boy whose diagram
was criticized had been solving a spatial problem, even
though its terms were not those given by the teacher. The
teacher must find herself divided between clarifying tasks
so that they can be comprehended by the first two, and
following up issues raised by the latter. Preliminary
planning helps with the former, but obscures the latter.

(d) Teacher supplies structure

The plight of children who have difficulty in making
reasoning explicit can be helped by a method some teachers
use, apparently without being aware of it.

Several examples occur in Lesson G (1966; physics;
comprehensive school). Of all the teachers whose lessons

we have studied this teacher showed himself most aware of the gulf between his frame of reference and that of his pupils, and devoted his very considerable teaching skill to enabling his pupils to join in his own way of thinking and talking. Having talked about air pressure in terms of a model barometer, he moves out into other applications of the same ideas, first to 'spacemen' and then – in the course of the passage quoted below – to 'mountaineers'. (Several sentences identifying mountaineers have been omitted from the middle of the passage.)

T   He carries an air supply because. . . ? Why does he need an air supply?
P   There isn't any air.
T   Good. There isn't any air. . . . Where there's no air . . . come on, complete it . . . well?
P   Life.
T   If you've got no air you've got no. . . ?
P   Air pressure.
T   No air pressure. . . . So what must mountaineers do if they find there's no air pressure?
     [Three sentences omitted here]
T   The reason why they want to have air cylinders is because. . . ?
P   There isn't any air, sir.
T   Good. There isn't much air.

Here the teacher supplies the linguistic structure that represents causal or other links between statements, and the pupils are required to have so far followed the teacher's reasoning as to be able to supply one statement of the linked pair. This seems particularly relevant to the teaching of rational sequences which the teacher wishes to hand over in a predetermined form. Since the pupils are required to contribute, certain kinds of gulf between the teacher's intentions and the pupil's comprehension will quickly show themselves. Notice that one pupil has failed to follow the teacher's thought and completes 'If you've got no air pressure you've got no . . .' with the word 'life'. The emotion-charged link of 'air' with 'life' has interposed itself before the link with pressure. The question whether the teacher should have followed up this dead-end must be determined by principles irrelevant to the present discussion.

The tact with which the teacher in his last speech substitutes 'much' for 'any' is also worth noticing. He is able thereby to correct a misstatement without detracting from his expression of approval. It may not be necessary to bring such errors to conscious notice. This might be analogous to the very young child who does not so much 'correct errors' in his language behaviour as gradually analyse and assimilate the patterns of adult language. This teacher seems to be operating – no doubt intuitively – upon the assumption that if his pupils can take part in a dialogue about his subject they will gradually be able to take over some of the structure of that dialogue into their own thinking.

Mathematics lessons provided similar examples. In Lesson J (1967) the teacher was drawing on the blackboard the diagram:

T   I've asked you how many thirds in a half [Working at blackboard] . . . so I could say that that's my third, couldn't I. . . . Right, and what else do I need to finish off my half. . . . I've got a gap left that I've got to fill in. . . . That's a whole third [pointing]. This is. . . ?
P   Half.
T   Half a. . . ?
P   Third.

The pupils thus become participants in the rational process.

(e) Demand for explicitness

It is now appropriate to move away from the teacher's duty to make publicly explicit to his pupils the criteria he is using. We now consider the function for the pupil of asking him to spell out explicitly what he is doing, thinking and learning. In effect, we are asking whether our material gives any evidence of what value it is to a pupil's learning if he is required to find words to express what he is learning – words, that is, which make available to him the structure of whatever it is he is learning. 'Knowing' can mean anything from being able to tick the right item in a multiple-choice question to being able to use whatever has been learnt to generate new insights. And in any new piece of learning it seems likely that the pupil has to make some progress along this continuum of insight. For example, in mathematics the pupils need to progress from being able to carry out a process to being able to make the process itself the subject of their perception. (This seems to be related to Piaget's 'concrete' and 'formal' operations.) To find means of representing a process to oneself is to bring it under conscious control.

Something of this can be seen in a sequence from Lesson A (1966; second-year mathematics; grammar school).

T   One divided by a quarter . . . what does that mean? Somebody express that in everyday language.

P   Quarter of one.

T   Is it a quarter of one? What's a quarter of one?

P   A quarter.

T   A quarter. It's not going to be more than that? What is it then? Yes, Farley?

P   Sir, it's one plus a quarter.

T   It's what?

P   One plus a quarter.

T   That is one plus a quarter is it? [writing on blackboard] I thought *that* was one plus a quarter. And that?

P   Sir.

T   What's this one? . . . What's it mean? Yes. . . ?

P   One divided by a quarter.
T   It's one divided by a quarter. What does one divided by a quarter mean? Yes. . . ?
P   How many quarters are there in one.
T   How many quarters are there in one. Well, if you think of it like that, 'How many quarters are there in one? How many quarters *are* there in one? Yes, Brooke?
P   Four, sir.
T   Yes, there are four.

These pupils, a year older than the others, are being asked not merely to operate the process of division by fractional numbers, but to become aware of the process. The teacher deals with each false suggestion not by saying that it is wrong but by demonstrating what follows from it. When a child suggests that one divided by a quarter is equivalent to a quarter of one he replies, 'It's not going to be more than that?' And similarly with the child who suggests 'One plus a quarter.' The whole tendency is to force these pupils, who have already added, multiplied and divided fractions, to make the process of division itself the object of perception, and to distinguish it from the process of multiplication and the process of addition.

It seems that the pupil who offered 'One plus a quarter' was at a very different stage of development from the child who was able to say, 'How many quarters are there in one.' The latter is clearly ready to perceive and manipulate abstract forms and processes. What happens is that the teacher accepts this latter contribution as the climax of the instructional sequence: he has made a 'right answer'; the point has been 'made'. Similarly in other lessons, the one child's answer is allowed to represent an achieved end, when the teacher can hardly know whether other pupils have reached the same level of comprehension. For example, in Lesson B (1966; mathematics; secondary modern) the teacher who is introducing the idea of co-ordinates, asks the class to draw the diagram on p. 42. Then he establishes by questions that when x is 2, then y is 2, and so on. Finally he asks: 'Can anybody tell

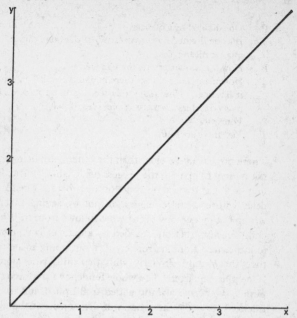

me how I can write that down on the blackboard in a kind
of shorthand way?' and when one pupil replies, '*x* equals
y' treats this as clinching the sequence.

In both of these cases the teacher was asking children
to verbalize very abstract processes, and this was clearly
very valuable to part of the class, at the very least. What is
also worthy of note is the teacher's need for a climactic
explicitness before he can leave the sequence. These
examples demand the question: if one child benefits from
making the conclusion explicit, would not others? And
this can be related to the point made above, that the
teacher should be careful to make explicit to the pupil
the criteria by which the pupil's performance will be
judged. Although our competencies often show themselves
in performance which is controlled intuitively, if we wish
to be able to control or change our performance we need
to be consciously aware of it. And we become aware of

performance by representing it to ourselves, either through language or through other symbolic systems.

A quite different kind of explicitness was sought by the teacher of Lesson D (1966; geography; girls' grammar school). The class was looking at a photograph of sand-dunes.

T   Sand dunes. They're usually in an unusual . . . a specific shape . . . a special shape. . . . Does anybody know what shape they are? Not in straight lines. . .

P   They're like hills.

T   Yes, they're like low hills.

P   They're all humpy up and down.

T   Yes, they're all humpy up and down.

P   They're like waves.

T   Good, they're like waves.

P   They're like . . .

T   They're a special shape.

P   They're like boulders . . . sort of go up and down getting higher and higher.

T   I don't know about getting higher and higher.

P   Something like pyramids.

T   Mm . . . wouldn't call them pyramids, no.

P   They're in a semi-circle.

T   Ah, that's getting a bit nearer. They're often in a semi-circle and nearly always . . . we call them . . . well, it's part of a semi-circle. . . . What do we call part of a semi-circle? You think of the moon . . . perhaps you'll get the shape.

P   Water.

T   No, not shaped like water. . . . Yes?

P   An arc.

T   An arc . . . oh, we're getting ever so much nearer.

P   Crescent.

T   A crescent shape. Have you heard that expression . . . a crescent shape? I wonder if anybody could draw me a crescent shape on the board. Yes, they're nearly all that shape. . . .

Although the teacher seems from the first to have been looking for the verbal label, 'crescent', in the course of searching for it language was used in quite other ways

than in merely offering a series of labels for rejection or
acceptance. At first the girls, who had a picture (and
probably some personal experience) to start from, took
the question as an invitation to *make this experience explicit*.
Thus we have 'like hills', 'like waves', 'sort of go up and
down getting higher and higher', and the strikingly
evocative 'all humpy up and down'. They are not taking
the shared experience of shape as given and finding a
name for it; they are exploring *what meaning any agreed
name should have*. But 'like pyramids' turns the class
towards the labelling function of language, so that 'in a
semi-circle', having earned the teacher's approval,
directs the class towards 'arc' and 'crescent'.

Would the class have gained as much if the name
'crescent' had come as an immediate answer to the first
question? What did they gain? Why is this the only case
in twelve lessons when the personal meaning of a word
was explored? Does this represent a significant lack in
the learning experience of younger secondary pupils, or
is this merely a chance bias of the small sample? What
function has language like 'all humpy up and down' for
the child who used it? Is it the vestige of something to be
outgrown, or the unformed promise of something to
come? This single example can raise these questions but
not answer them.

(f) Pupil-initiated sequences

When another adult gives us new information we may or
may not question him. This seems to be determined by
our assessment of the role we are playing at that moment,
and especially by our role-relationship with the speaker.
One would therefore expect that in the classroom, where
the pupil's role as learner and the teacher's role as mediator
are so well defined, questioning of the teacher by the
pupils would take a large part of lesson time, side by side
with presentation and application activities. Yet any
teacher knows that this is not so. Why, then, do our
pupils not actively ask questions that would help bridge

the gulf between their frame of reference and that of the teacher?

Our sample supported teachers' impressions. We excluded cases where an open question by the teacher (e.g. 'What does the desert have to exchange?') calls forth a diversity of suggestions, each of which has to be dealt with separately. We included only cases where a pupil had of his own accord raised a new issue, either by an unsolicited statement, or by a question. This definition of 'pupil-initiated sequences' made it possible to separate out twenty examples from the twelve lessons. These included:

3 requests for information for its own sake
4 requests for information to confirm an insight
1 request for a theoretical explanation
6 questions about the method of carrying out a task
6 statements
—
20 total
—

The questions about practical methods are different in kind from the others (e.g. 'Can we use *deep* pencil?' i.e. heavy shading). They seem to have two functions: the child is not so much wanting information as reassurance; but at the same time the questions tend to turn all tasks into right/wrong tasks, performance in which can be judged against an objective norm. This may reflect a teacher's unspoken assumptions: in Lesson M a child, told to write a limerick, asks, 'Can I put "The chief defect of myself"?' The teacher, by choosing the limerick and emphasizing its metrical pattern, has 'taught' the child that – at least in this case – her language behaviour can be put up against a model and judged right or wrong. That is, even these requests for practical advice appear to function as part of the child's learning, and can give investigators information about it.

The requests for information fall into two parts: some appear to be merely fact gathering. The teacher has taught a coherent body of facts, but the pupil has perceived them as separate, and is asking for more. But other requests for information show that a pupil has gained an insight and wishes to test it; in two cases these insights were not relevant to what the teacher was teaching. What the teacher teaches is not the same as what the pupil learns. All of the six 'statements' were sharply relevant, and in two cases they corrected errors made by teachers.

So perhaps nine of these sequences show pupils engaging in learning as actively as intelligent adults do. This is so minute a part of the total time of the twelve lessons as to challenge further attention.

The Language of Instruction

This section concerns itself with the 'registers', or sets of language forms, used by teachers when they are dealing with the material and processes of their subject. It is also concerned with teachers' awareness or unawareness of these choices of register. These concerns distinguish this section from that which follows, which deals with the language by which the teacher controls the personal interactions of the classroom.

The language of instruction will be dealt with under three headings:

(a) *Specialist language presented*. This includes language forms special to the teacher's subject which he is aware of as a potential barrier to his pupils' understanding, and which he therefore 'presents' to them with deliberate care.

(b) *Specialist language not presented*. Language forms special to the subject may not be deliberately 'presented' to pupils either (i) because they have previously been introduced, or (ii) because the teacher is not aware that he is using them. (Since the samples were taken in the sixth week of the pupils' secondary education examples of the latter are likely to be far more numerous.)

(c) *The language of secondary education.* This includes language forms not specific to any school subject, and which pupils would not normally hear or use in speech. (In associating this register of language with secondary education it is not suggested that it cannot be found in some primary school classrooms.)

These three categories have been described in impressionistic terms because no operational definitions exist. The sample can be used for three purposes: it can be used to show that these categories have some sort of objective reality; it can display some of the language found in each category; it can allow us to raise some of the pedagogical implications of these specializations of teachers' language.

(a) Specialist language presented

It would not be true to say that teachers are unaware that language plays a part in learning. The eleven teachers in the sample were sharply aware of certain aspects of the language they used – and to some extent expected their pupils to use – in managing their subject matter. It is important to notice the unanimity with which teachers perceive one part of language and fail to perceive the rest; the study demonstrated this beyond doubt. (This may be related to the age at which the teachers themselves achieved this part of their linguistic competence; what we learn before we are able to represent it to ourselves is usually very difficult to make conscious.)

Teachers are aware of certain of the technical terms which they use, showing this by what we shall call 'presenting' the terms. 'Presentation' will sometimes imply that a term is supplied by the teacher and a definition asked for, and at other times that the teacher explicitly gives a name, or asks pupils to give a name, to a concept which has already been established. (In the sample, the pupils were asked to supply a term or a definition three times as often as the teacher supplied them.) For example, in Lesson F (chemistry; grammar school) the words 'chromatography', 'pestle and mortar', 'suspension', 'effluent' and 'chlorophyll' were presented to the class. Examples were much less common in the lessons from non-selective schools, with the sole exception of Lesson K (history) which presented 'city states', 'patriotic', 'inquiring mind', 'language', 'truce', and 'pentathlon'. It will be noted that these are mainly nouns. Neither in science nor maths lessons could a systematic policy be perceived, either in the selection of concepts to be taught or in the order of presentation of the concept and a term to represent it.

Indeed, in many of the twenty-five examples examined it is hard to say what value could come either from defining a term or in providing a term for a concept which pupils had already verbalized successfully. An extreme case occurred in Lesson F.

T   We're going to cut the grass into small pieces and then we're going to put it into the . . . what we call a mortar . . . this is what we call a mortar . . . this bowl . . . and anyone know what we call the other thing which we're going to pound it in?

The act of giving a technical name seems for many teachers to have taken on a value of its own in separation from its utility; in this case the naming activity is totally irrelevant to the process which it interrupts.

Later in the same lesson the teacher, his attention upon purposeless name teaching, fails to notice a pupil whose reply shows his incomprehension.

T   Now I don't know whether any of you could jump the gun a bit and tell me what actually is this green stuff which produces green colour. . . .
P   Er . . . um . . . water.
T   No. . . . Have you heard of chlorophyll?

The pupil's reply should have warned the teacher that there were children in the class to whom he was communicating nothing. (When seen in the total context of the lesson, the child's reply must mean no less than this.)

This makes the teacher's wish to teach the word 'chlorophyll' doubly irrelevant. His desire to teach terminology prevents him from perceiving his true tasks.

In Lesson E (1966; biology; comprehensive school) also, the biological terminology seems to take a value of its own.

T   Where does it go then?

P   To your lungs, Miss.

T   Where does it go before it reaches your lungs? . . . Paul.

P   Your windpipe, Miss.

T   Down the windpipe. . . . Now can anyone remember the other word for windpipe?

P   The trachea.

T   The trachea . . . good. . . . After it has gone through the trachea where does it go to then? . . . There are a lot of little pipes going into the lungs . . . what are those called? . . . Ian?

P   The bronchii.

T   The bronchii . . . that's the plural. . . . What's the singular? What is one of these tubes called? . . . Ann.

P   Bronchus.

T   Bronchus . . . with 'us' at the end. . . . What does 'inspiration' mean. . . ?

This too is an extreme case, which underlines an assumption shared in some degree by six of the twelve teachers; the teaching of terminology is seen as part of the task. It is clear from the substitution of 'trachea' for 'windpipe' that it is not merely the referential function of the word that is valued; the teacher is valuing that of the two synonyms which carries with it (for her, not the pupils, of course) the stronger suggestion of a strictly biological context.

Some teachers find a greater propriety in the familiar specialist term. The teacher of religious knowledge in Lesson N (1967) said men pray to God 'because God controls the earth . . . because he controls the weather . . . so that the food can grow that we are able to have it . . . God *provides* . . . is the word . . . God provides this food

for us. ...' When he says '"provides" ... is the word'
he is demonstrating a right/wrong view of the relationship
of a word to its referent which might well be questioned.

Two examples of presentation have been quoted above
in the section on 'pupil participation': a discussion of the
shape of sand-dunes leading to the presentation of
'crescent' (p. 43), and the investigation of the meaning
for the pupils of the word 'language' (p. 29) in which
their use of the term limited it to spoken language. The
first of these was quoted as an example of valuable classroom discussion; very few of the other twenty-four
examples of presentation could be quoted approvingly
for that purpose. Some of the sequences are puzzling:

T   Would anyone like to give us a definition [of a fraction]?
P.1 Part of a whole number.
T   Yes, part of a whole number. ... Yes?
P.2 ... [inaudible] the numerator of that denominator.
T   It consists. ... What did you call it? ... It consists of two
     parts, er ... numerator and the denominator, er, used in
     fact for dividing. ...

The teacher appears to give equal approval to both
answers, though we may assume that the first was what
was wanted. It might be questioned whether either 'definition' had any function for the children in revising, as they
were, the division and multiplication of fractions.

Later in Lesson A the teacher asks:

T   Now what in fact does it mean when we say 'three times
     six'? Yes, Jameson?
P   Three multiplied by six.
T   It means three multiplied by six.

The teacher seems satisfied, but it is hard to imagine
what function such a substitution could be conceived to
have. The teacher confuses the ability to substitute one
term for another with the ability to use the words to
think with.

The kind of awareness shown by teachers in their presentation of specialist language should by now have been
sufficiently illustrated. The technical term is often taken

to have a value of its own, and its substitution for an alternative formulation is sometimes taken to have the weight of an explanation.

(b) Specialist language not presented

The range of technical language (that is, language special to a curricular subject) of which teachers are sufficiently aware to present in this way is limited, as will have been seen. Side by side with these presentations, some teachers are using specialist language without explicitly presenting it.

Some of these were technical terms of the subject which are well enough known to be unlikely to present difficulty; in an English lesson 'stress' and 'rhyme'; in physics 'diagram' and 'pulley'; in mathematics 'point'; in history 'a major city'.

Others were as much part of the teacher's idiolect as part of the subject register; one mathematics teacher used 'split' repeatedly, whereas another used 'sliced' and 'divided' in similar contexts. (Mathematics lessons appear to have a register of their own, quite separate from the register of mathematics proper.) With these might be classed 'pointer' (physics), 'an unhappy ending' (English), and others.

All these examples come from non-selective schools; they are few and trivial enough for their effect upon the children's learning to be ignored. But when we turn to one of the lessons from grammar schools we find that language of this kind bulks more large. This is the chemistry lesson (F); we have already quoted the passage in which a teacher tries to explain that milk is 'a suspension of very fine particles together with water'. Almost every sentence contains similar subject-specific terms. A more extreme example is:

T   Put that into the distillation flask and then distil off and then we get thermometer recording the correct temperature which is the boiling point for acetone. Then we collect the acetone which came over as a distillate.

This teacher showed that he had difficulty in thinking of his subject without using its terminology. In the passage quoted below he wishes to say that it would be possible to extract all the colour from grass by using a more complex form of his method, but was unable to free himself from the phrase 'under reflux conditions' enough to realize that he had already said enough with 'using a different method'.

T   If we did it using a different method actually . . . where we heat up the grass with acetone actually . . . heating it under, er . . . an enclosed system except . . . I'll have to show using a diagram on that . . . well er . . . under reflux conditions so that we didn't lose the acetone then we could actually finish up with the grass a white colour.

It can be surmised that this teacher's enthusiasm for his subject and his abundance of knowledge tended to stop him from perceiving his pupils' needs. Talk of this kind would certainly discourage many pupils; it is tempting to make guesses about which pupils would be best able to tolerate such language and to continue to attend to it until such time as they could begin to take part. It was shown above (p. 28) that at least two boys were beginning to be able to take part. For these two, the dialogue with the teacher must have been exciting; for the others it is likely to have been a painful demonstration of their inadequacy.

Not all grammar school teachers are as extreme as this. Lesson C (history) and Lesson D (geography) show much less use of unpresented technical terminology. In this they were little different from the lessons from non-selective schools. (It must be remembered, however, that what is taught as history and geography in the first year of the secondary school bears little relationship to the questions debated by academic historians and geographers, so that the teacher is less likely to bring in the terminology of his own academic studies than is the case in scientific subjects.)

The quotations from the grammar school chemistry lesson can be compared with those from the biology lesson (E) which showed a teacher in a comprehensive school who was much concerned with the *teaching* of terminology. (See pp. 34, 49 and 70.) It can be argued that this biology teacher was giving her pupils more support than the chemistry teacher was giving to his pupils. Although the biology teacher used terms such as 'the human respiratory system', she can be presumed to have 'presented' these to the class in an earlier lesson.

Thus it does not appear that in most lessons the un-planned use of specialist language unfamiliar to the pupils is likely to be a major problem. The grammar school chemistry lesson is, however, in most striking contrast to this; it would be useful to know how often such lessons happen in grammar schools, in which subjects, and whether their frequency increases as pupils grow older.

(c) The language of secondary education

It is in discussing the third category, called here 'the language of secondary education', that the lack of an objective method of circumscribing the material will most obtrude. The register referred to has much in common with the language of textbooks, of official publications, of almost any printed document that sets out to discuss a topic in an impersonal public way, and indeed with the language in which this paper is expressed. The register, being a spoken one, overlaps still more with the language of public debate and discussion in which the business of the community is carried on, in meetings and committees of greater or less formality. Martin Joos called such a register the 'consultative style' and C. H. Barber in examining scientific writing found elements of this register and referred to them as 'stylistic variations'. We are here referring to an enormous and complex area of socio-linguistic behaviour. It is clear that all men and women who wish to take a full part in social life need kinds of explicit public language which fall within this area. What is in question is the part that varieties of this language should play in the classroom.

An analysis (into the three categories) of the language of seven lessons from non-selective schools quickly made it clear that the relationship of one category to another could not be expressed in numerical terms. The language of secondary education was not just a matter of unfamiliar words that could be counted; nor did any other objective unit offer itself. It was necessary to fall back upon a subjective impression supported by examples. In the lessons from non-selective schools, specialist terms, presented or not, were infrequent; most of the teachers, however, used many terms which, while not specialist, would not be part of the language of their pupils' every-day living. Lessons from selective schools were even more dominated by this language of secondary education, as even a cursory reading showed.

This implies that if we speak of 'the language of history lessons' or of 'the language of physics lessons' we are more likely to be considering forms of language which are shared by these than forms which are specific to one or other of them. But it is not this dominant register of language which teachers are aware of; rather teachers perceive the specialist terms which they 'present'. It follows that they are not taking responsibility for their use of such a register, and are unaware of any problems which its use may add to their pupils' tasks in learning.

Another way of looking at this register, then, is to see it as including those non-specialist forms of language which are outside the normal experience of eleven-year-old pupils. The linguistic experience of eleven-year-olds must, however, vary so much that this formulation is of little use except to emphasize that a lesson largely couched in such language will be beyond many pupils' comprehension.

We illustrate a teacher's unawareness of the language of secondary education from Lesson K (1967); the teacher, who is not a history specialist, used the phrase 'city states', paused, and then defined it:

T   They were called 'city states' because they were complete in themselves. . . . They were governed by themselves . . . ruled by themselves . . . they supported themselves [short omission]. . . . These states were complete in themselves because the terrain between cities was so difficult that it was hard for them to communicate. . . . Now because these people lived like this in their own cities they tended to be intensely patriotic towards their own city. . . . Now what's 'patriotic' mean?

What is notable here is not so much an obvious blunder such as 'terrain' but that in trying to explain 'city states' the teacher seems unable to escape from language equally unfamiliar to children: 'complete in themselves', 'ruled by themselves', 'supported themselves', 'communicate', 'tended to be'. 'City states' is typical of the kind of concept which teachers are enough aware of to 'present' to pupils; the other phrases exemplify the language of secondary education, which this teacher was so unaware of that he used it to explain the former. It is not until he reaches 'patriotic' that he recognizes another concept which needs presentation. Concepts such as 'complete in themselves' or 'tended to be' may carry less meaning to the child than does 'patriotic', which can easily be linked with something he knows. One set of counters is being substituted for another; words are being shown to be equivalent to words; and it is left to the pupils to summon up some kind of meaning for them. In learning such essential concepts as 'tendency', which form part of no specialism, the child is given no support from school, which tacitly assumes that he comprehends them. Children whose home life does not support such language learning may feel themselves to be excluded from the conversation in the classroom.

Is the register merely a random group of forms, or can it be shown to have any structure? In the small sample available only three items recur, the single words 'similar', 'explain' and 'complicated'; no categorization of larger structures seems possible. This seems at first glance to be the result of the smallness of the sample, but a larger sample would be no better. There is no reason why the items should fall into formal categories: it is not useful to regard the register as a set of lexical or syntactic items; it is the function of the item which is significant, not its form. And if it is the function which is significant, then any structure will be a structure of the on-going classroom interaction in which the forms have their functions.

Harold Rosen suggests (in the passage quoted, pp. 11-12) that in considering a specialized language 'we should set about distinguishing between the linguistic-conventional and the linguistic-intellectual'. These two categories distinguish two kinds of function: the 'linguistic-conventional' functions, which correspond to what we shall call the 'socio-cultural' functions, are concerned with identifying the speaker's role and his relationship with his interlocutors; the 'linguistic-intellectual' functions are conceptual in nature, carrying the essential thought processes of the lesson. Thus we might distinguish two categories:

(i) *Socio-cultural.* Here the language forms may be signalling to the speaker himself, and to his interlocutors, that he is segmenting reality as a physicist, or more largely as a scientist, or as a member of a committee, or as a participant in a public meeting. For any individual, the registers expand in concentric circles from forms which indicate a widely available social role to forms which indicate a limited subject-specialism. (For the same individual there could be contrasted another concentric set of registers related to his domestic roles.) This suggests that no clear-cut division will be possible *within the socio-cultural functions* between the register of a specialism and the register of secondary education.

(ii) *Conceptual.* Similar sets of concentric circles can be imagined when the language used is also carrying conceptual processes. The specialized registers on the periphery could be distinguished from the general registers at the centre by the relative degree of agreement between interlocutors about what the words mean.

Difficulties arise, however, when we apply these two categories to the register of secondary education in the sample of lessons. Certain cases fall clearly into the 'socio-cultural' category:

'is still quite apparent today' (K)
'The point I would like to make is' (L)
'prepare the evening meal' (N)
'from exhaustion' (G)

If these were phrased differently ('because they were tired' for 'from exhaustion'), this would not alter that part of the meaning which relates to the subject matter, but only that part which relates to the speaker's attitude to his present role.

Other cases fall clearly into the 'conceptual' category:

'a civilization ... better developed' (K)
'something in common' (M)
'present together in that proportion' (L)
'the position of ... in relation to ...' (B)

These differ in that, *for the speaker*, a change in the terminology would be a change in that part of the meaning which relates to the subject matter. But *for most pupils* the phrases would not have this precise meaning; the precise relationships implied in 'developed', 'in common', 'proportion', and 'relation' would be likely to carry a far more *generalized* significance for them. Thus, although the two categories properly describe aspects of the teacher's *production* of these utterances, the pupils may be receiving all of them as socio-cultural in nature. These considerations should be kept in mind during the discussion which follows.

Only a proportion of the items fall without any doubt into one or other of these two categories. For example, 'if you are ever faced with' implies a problem-solving model for experience, but can be taken as a socio-cultural variant only. ('If you are ever faced with a room where gas is present, never ever take a match to the room where it is coming from.') Even the word 'explain', which for the teacher means something like 'Make a logical statement about causes within the implied framework of the subject', is treated by many children as if it meant 'Make any statement relevant to the matter in hand'. (We might ask ourselves by what processes a child becomes not only able to make his statements acceptable to the teacher as socially appropriate, but also internalize the teacher's conceptual frame so that what the pupil says means the same to him as it does to the teacher.) When a teacher says 'what position the mark is in', what does this mean to his pupils? All will be used in dealing with marks which are here and marks which are there, but the teacher is requiring them to abstract the concept of 'position' from a diversity of past manipulation of marks on various materials. Their ability to do this must vary from child to child.

When the teacher asks 'How many pieces does that cake *consist of*?' is he using 'consist of' merely because it is habitual to his role of mathematics teacher, or does it remind him of certain assumptions about the possibility of numerical analysis of physical phenomena? Clearly in this case the conceptual content is latent: by using 'does that cake consist of' rather than 'has that cake been cut into' the teacher holds his own mental processes within a frame within which many latent mathematical concepts are available.

Two conclusions follow. From the point of view of the teacher, everything he says has for him a more or less important socio-cultural function in supporting his roles as teacher and as teacher-of-mathematics; yet everything he says could also (in theory) be placed on a scale for its conceptual function, according to how far it is also being used to organize the subject matter of the lesson. But this is only for the teacher; for the pupil it must be different.

Each new item must first appear to the pupil to have a socio-cultural function – that is, to be 'the sort of thing my physics teacher says' – and then, in so far as the pupil is able to use the item in talking, thinking or writing, it will take upon itself a conceptual function.

All this applies as much to subject-specific language as to the language of secondary education. Experienced teachers are able to help their pupils to use subject-specific language. The language of secondary education provides a different problem, partly because it is more pervasive, and partly because teachers are less aware of it.

The register of secondary education played some part in all the lessons of the sample. All the examples so far quoted have come from lessons in non-selective schools, and even amongst these the teachers varied widely in extent to which they used the register. (No attempt has been made to measure the relative predominance of the register in each of the lessons, since such a measure would almost certainly be meaningless.) The investigators agreed that within the 1966 sample there was distinctly more use of the register in grammar school lessons than in non-selective school lessons, though even here there was variation: the teacher in Lesson F (chemistry) stayed in the register almost throughout the instructional exchanges of the lesson, whereas the teacher in Lessons C and D moved into it only every few sentences. In Lesson F, however, the register is interpenetrated by the specialist terminology of chemistry, as can be seen in the example quoted earlier in this section. In lessons C and D, the register carries less specialized conceptual processes, and is generally more free of specialist terminology:

T   The nature of the land together with the climate really controlled what was grown on Crete and what sort of occupations the people on the island performed.

Thus any conclusions arrived at about the effect on learning of the language of secondary education must apply to all schools in the sample, but more strongly to the selective schools.

This linguistic register can be assumed to affect learning in two ways: when it is being used to manipulate the concepts being taught, it may help or hinder the learning; its relative predominance in a lesson must be seen solely as a hindrance, since it is likely to influence adversely some pupils' ability to identify their purposes with those of the teacher. Thus it may be hypothesized that, if this register is as widely used as the limited evidence suggests, no child who cannot learn to manage it (in one sense or another) can hope to take much part in secondary education. This leaves us with two pedagogical questions. How far is the language of secondary education necessary to the teaching of secondary school subjects? How can pupils be best helped to learn that part which is necessary? This is not the place to suggest what answers to these questions would be like.

It may well be asked whether the language of secondary education is co-terminous with Bernstein's 'elaborated code'. This seems not to be the case. Amongst the characteristics Bernstein postulates for his elaborated code is that it is used to make explicit the uniqueness of individual intention. Now while the register we are considering is capable of a complexity and explicitness which would allow for such functions, we are not asserting that it is always used in this way. Its predictability varies with the person using it. Bernstein's codes are concerned rather with ways of using language than with groups of language forms, though he has shown that the former can in some ways influence the frequency of the latter. Almost all the language used by secondary teachers in their lessons will tend towards the elaborated code partly because teachers are isolated by their status, and partly because many see themselves as handing over an explicitly formulated body of learning. Bernstein's thesis would direct attention to those *uses* of language likely to be unfamiliar to pupils, rather than towards unfamiliar *forms*.

This distinction is of extreme importance to any

pedagogical choices in the teaching of the language needed by secondary pupils in their learning as a whole. Part of the business of secondary education is to help pupils to abstract from the relatively undifferentiated codification of experience represented by the language of everyday social intercourse those special recodifications of aspects of the same experience which belong to subjects such as physics or economics. The abundant evidence here for a more general register suggests that, in order to be able to take part in these special recodifyings, secondary pupils must also recodify reality along dimensions shared by many or all of these subjects. Although these recodifications may be described in terms of linguistic registers, learning to codify experience in these ways will be a matter of far more than learning new language forms. Any teacher knows of pupils who have learnt whole stretches of a new register which they can put together only in ways which demonstrate that they are not using the language as symbols for new dimensions along which to locate their experiences. Thus the teacher's task should not be to introduce a new set of linguistic forms, but to help his pupils to use language to organize experience in a new way.

Here lies the importance of pupil participation. It is when the pupil is required to use language to grapple with new experience or to order old experience in a new way that he is most likely to find it necessary to use language differently. And this will be very different from taking over someone else's language in external imitation of its forms: on the contrary, it is the first step towards new patterns of thinking and feeling, new ways of representing reality to himself. Thus Bernstein's distinction helps us to see why classroom interaction is important. It is not enough for pupils to imitate the forms of teachers' language as if they were models to be copied; it is only when they 'try it out' in reciprocal exchanges so that they modify the way they use language to organize reality that they are able to find new functions for language in thinking and feeling. This would suggest that the low level of pupil participation in these lessons, if they are at all typical of secondary lessons, is a matter of some educational urgency. All teachers might well contemplate the classroom implications of this.

Language and Classroom Control

Information from this study about the relationship between styles of language and styles of teacher–pupil interaction has proved sparse. The sample is too small, undoubtedly, but it may well be that a study such as this is not the best way of gathering such information.

Several investigators have said of the lessons which they witnessed and transcribed that what were significant were the patterns of stress, intonation, and so on. This is, of course, to be expected, since much of our adjustment to one another in any groups is carried out through these aspects of language. None of the investigators has, unfortunately, been capable of the kind of analysis which might have substantiated this. The investigator responsible for lesson J (1967; mathematics) was impressed by the variety of intonations which the teacher gave to the word 'right', used partly to mark the close of one sequence and to direct attention to another, but also to hold attention and to emphasize that it was she who was directing the sequences.

We are not concerned only with what most teachers would first take 'controlling a class' to refer to. We have already pointed out (p. 37) that pupils have to learn to filter out of all the language washing over them those utterances which will need to be acted upon, or which carry important statements. That is, they must learn to operate a differential attentiveness. What would be very interesting would be to find from those pupils who have mastered this what signals they respond to. Experienced teachers often indicate the need for special attention by a change of intonation which outside the classroom would sound abnormal. (For various reasons this is often more marked with primary school teachers.) This seems also to be one function of the 'right' used in Lesson J and by many other teachers. Pupils' ability thus to differentiate their attentiveness may have a marked effect upon their success in school.

A teacher establishes his relationship with his pupils – their mutual expectations, that is – more in instructional sequences than in the small proportion of sequences overtly concerned with social control. Thus it is not enough to consider the relationship between language, teacher–pupil relationships and learning only in sequences which are solely concerned with social control. The language of the teacher enacts for the child the relevance of the lesson. We have already quoted (on p. 43) a sequence from Lesson D in which the teacher allows her pupils, almost by accident, to explore with words the shape of sand dunes on the way to choosing 'crescent shape' to describe them. ('All humpy up and down', etc.) This teacher, though in general she used the language of secondary education, was also able to speak informally. 'Pop it in the oven' and 'Can't half make you jump' contrast notably with her usual lecturing style. Like several other teachers, she was aware how unfamiliar much of what she was teaching must seem to her pupils. On the whole she dealt with this by supplying an abundance of details, but upon several occasions she used familiar comparisons: 'It gets terribly hot during the day ... so hot that you could fry an egg on the rocks.' Speaking of marking tracks in a sand-desert she said:

T   If you go from here to Manchester over the top road over the Pennines ... over the hills ... you'll find that across the roads ... um on the road ... along the roads there are poles put by the side of the road so that when the road is covered over with snow the tops of the poles remain above ... then you can find your way. Any of you seen the poles over the moors? Oh, some of you. Well, the same sort of thing happens in the desert. ...

A similar sequence occurs in Lesson G (1966; physics; comprehensive school). Having demonstrated with apparatus that a greater weight of air above causes greater pressure in the air below, the teacher wishes his pupils to apply this to places they know.

T   If I put three barometers . . . one on top of Norland Moor, one at school . . . and one right in the middle of Blackpool Promenade . . . which one . . . now you've got to think this out . . . which one would go up the furtherest because it's the biggest pressure. . . ?

For all its colloquial qualities this passage is extremely precise and well adjusted to its purposes. (Some teachers may disagree about its precision, but we should not allow this to divert attention from its function in helping the children to take part in the lesson.) The colloquial flexibility and informality of this teacher's style establishes a warm social interchange which invites pupils to contribute. By retaining something of the warmth and improvisatory quality of lively everyday speech, he encourages pupils to feel that what they can bring from their own lives is relevant to what is being talked about. They too can use language to grope for new meanings, to sort out experience for themselves. This is perhaps the most important idea which has arisen from the discussion of these lessons: that the crucial quality of a teacher's language is whether it is warm, exploratory, available, encouraging the child to involve himself actively in the learning, or whether it is cold, inflexible, defensive, and discouraging.

The Predominance of Language

In both 1966 and 1967 the investigators were surprised at the predominance of language in the lessons. In four mathematics lessons and one English lesson the blackboard was used, but in only one case (to be quoted below) was it used other than as an illustration of oral exposition.

One maths teacher had prepared large diagrams on paper. In two physics lessons and one chemistry lesson the teacher demonstrated with apparatus, in all cases as the basis for a verbal exchange. Textbooks, including an atlas, were used in two history, one geography, and one religious education lesson; in the geography lesson a small picture in the book was discussed (see p. 43). That is, the study would suggest that 'chalk and talk' is still predominant in the classroom, except for one lesson. This is Lesson H, which for various reasons was not included in the transcription and analysis, and which was a drama lesson, taught in the school hall by the same teacher who taught Lesson M. This lesson consisted solely of individual or group improvisation; language entered only in the teacher's instructions, and the groups' discussion of their tasks.

In Lesson C (1966; history, grammar school) the teacher was seeking to give a picture of Minoan civilization. Well informed, and an exceptionally fluent speaker, she lectured to the class giving them what might be called 'word pictures'. Pupils played only a small part in her lessons.

T   The artists on the island of Crete showed the things of nature as nearly as possible as they saw them. . . . When the Egyptian artists painted they made things rather still and formal and er an Egyptian artist would paint a flower but the flower wouldn't look as if it was growing It would look as if it was cut out and still and stiff, whereas the Minoan artists showed a flower and you could almost feel that you could see it bending in the wind . . . it was painted in a much more graceful and natural way. . . .

For all this teacher's vividness ('cut out and still and stiff') and flexible variation of intonation and vocal quality, one cannot but feel that this would have been better done with the aid of pictures, and by the pupils talking more than the teacher.

It is not difficult to point to several passages like this one in which the teacher's intentions could probably have been carried out more effectively if visual or other materials had been available. Yet this does not seem to exhaust the implications of the domination of lessons by language – and mainly by the teacher's spoken language it should be noted. The domination seems to amount to an unintended restriction of the kinds of learning which can go on in the classroom. Pupils could take a more active part in manipulating materials, in planning and carrying out demonstrations, and in measuring and recording what they perceive. This is not to denigrate the function of language in learning: indeed, in these lessons the failure to demand active involvement of the pupils *has gone hand in hand with a failure to demand that they verbalize their learning*, that is, that they use language as an active instrument for reorganizing their perceptions. (This latter failure has been examined on pp. 26–34.) It is not that there is too much language, but that it is not fulfilling its functions as an instrument of learning. Rather, *language is seen as an instrument of teaching.*

It has already been suggested that the blackboard can be used in two ways: it can be used to illustrate the teacher's verbal exposition; in subjects where the matter taught can be represented upon a plane surface, it can be used to present a problem in visual terms. This latter use is illustrated by a sequence from a mathematics lesson (B) (1966; secondary modern). The teacher wishes the pupils to realize that in using co-ordinates to describe the position of a dot on the blackboard it is necessary to establish conventional agreement that the horizontal co-ordinate precedes the vertical or vice versa. He could have used this principle without making it explicit, and left the pupils to follow; he could have 'explained' the reasons to them; he chose to represent the need to them in visual terms as a problem to be solved.

T Now can you tell me what the position of the dot is in relation to those two lines? Glenys.

P Two, eight.

T Two, eight ... what does it mean 'two, eight'? What does it mean? ... All right ... Sandra.

P Two squares up ... eight squares across.

T	Two squares up; eight squares across . . . rub that one out . . . and put another one . . . and what is this one?
P	Six, three.
T	Six, three.
P	[another] Three, six.
T	Just so; three, six.
P	Three, six.
T	Is it?
P	Three, six.
T	That is quite right. . . . It could be three, six. . . . Why shouldn't it be? What do you mean by three, six?
P	Three squares from bottom; six squares across.
T	Is he right? If he said three, six and asked me to mark a dot on this blackboard [makes another dot on the blackboard] . . . points one three . . . six . . .
Ps	[Untranscribable chorus]
T	What must we do . . . to try to avoid confusion as to which of the two points is the right one? Can you, Janice?
P	Count the bottom squares first and then the side squares.
T	If everyone remembers these then there must be no doubt about it.

And there the teacher leaves the matter without making the principle any more explicit. It would probably have been useless to begin with general statements about the convention; the pupils could only have understood it as a rigid instruction imposed upon them. Because they had grappled at first-hand with the problem of translation from a spatial to a symbolic representation, the pupils had experienced the ambiguity and therefore the need for an 'order' morpheme in the symbolic system, and had at least the opportunity of understanding that its status was conventional, not rigid. (It could be argued that the teacher might usefully have asked the class to try to formulate a general statement; this cannot be decided here.) Moreover, this sequence avoided a fault already frequently illustrated in this paper, the fault of asking questions which fail to make explicit the criteria by which the answer will be judged. 'It could be three, six. . . . Why shouldn't it be ?' The child answering has to account for an ambiguity present to all the class; his responsibility is to this ambiguity, and not to unstated criteria guiding the teacher. This teacher has succeeded in objectifying his criteria into the terms of the problem he has presented to the class.

A distinction is here being made between two uses of language in the classroom. In one use language is the means by which knowledge is handed over; the knowledge is in verbal form, and when it requires explanation it is explained verbally. When a pupil is asked to use the knowledge to talk or write, he can organize his performance solely by an act of insight into the language performance of his teacher or his textbook; he has no recourse available to any non-verbal criteria to check his performance. Learning becomes heavily dependent upon the child's ability to take over by an act of imagination whatever linguistic constraints operate upon the teacher. In the other use, pointed to by the previous quotation, the exchange begins with a shared activity in which the nature of what is going on is openly available to the participants: all the children can comprehend the desire to communicate information about where the dot is, and have shared the discovery of ambiguity. Language here has the function of *making explicit to themselves* – as much as to other people – the nature of an insight already partly intuited.

These are two extremes; most of the language of the classroom must fall somewhere between. Yet to look at classroom exchanges in these terms may throw light upon certain failures of communication. In Lesson C the teacher interrupted her long description of Minoan civilization to ask:

T   What kind of knowledge must the Ancient Minoans have had to build a palace like the palace of Crete and to be able to organize a whole drainage system and so on?

P   They were very good at making things and building things.

T   Yes. . . . Now, in order to build something you can't just gather the er building materials together and um start putting it up, you have to plan. What sort of planning . . . what sort of knowledge do you need to be able to plan? Mary.

P   You have to be an architect really.

T   Yes. . . . Now, what kind of skill does an architect need? What kind of calculations does he have to make? He has to know what building material to use but also it's a question of how to use it.

P   Do you have to have geometrical knowledge?

T   He has to have a practical knowledge of maths doesn't he? [short omission] So there must have been architects living on Ancient Crete who had a practical grasp of the kind of maths needed to build a palace of this size and er magnificence.

At first glance we may assume that the question is too abstract for the class. They only reach the answer the teacher wants because she drops the clue 'calculations', and then it is – as far as we know – only one pupil who is able to use that. Why are they unable to answer the question? It is because they lack 'insight' into building in general, building as it occurs around them, that they cannot answer. The question is a meaningful and valuable one, but its answer would have to be based not merely on a verbal knowledge that stresses and weights have to be calculated, but upon the kind of knowledge that would imply visits to building sites and interviews with builders and civil engineers. Such knowledge would require a substantial and lengthy study which would finally give pupils an insight into the sophistication of Minoan building techniques. We are not, of course, saying that this should be a part of the school curriculum, but merely that the teacher of Lesson C inevitably failed to give this insight since she used words alone. An archaeologist to whom a length of excavated foundations means sophisticated building techniques did not learn this from purely verbal teaching. It is easy for teachers to deceive themselves about what they achieve in their lessons.

A similar failure to realize that for a child reality is

organized upon a different set of matrices, so that the same words mean something different, is displayed in Lesson K (1967; history).

T Tell me about Homer. . . . In what form did Homer write his stories?
P Attractive.
T Yes . . . it sounds nice. . . . There's a sort of rhythm . . . a flow about it. . . .

In this simpler example it is easy to isolate the word 'form' as the focus of misunderstanding, but could the matter be solved by a definition of 'form', as teachers sometimes seem to assume? In this case, the kind of knowledge which the teacher unconsciously assumes in his pupils would have necessitated more reading and writing of poetry and prose, *and discussion of their differences*, than is likely or perhaps possible by eleven years of age.

Let us now examine part of a biology lesson (E) (1966; grammar school) in which a teacher is trying to give a content to the terminology of her specialism.

T So the oxygen is taken to all parts of our body in the bloodstream. Now . . . how is it different in the insect? . . . Now, we did this in the last lesson . . . yes . . . ?
P Miss, it's got a lot of tubes in its body, Miss.
T The spider . . . er . . . insect has tubes running through its body. What are these tubes called?
P Trachea.
T Trachea. . . . Now, if an insect needs oxygen in a certain part of its body the oxygen goes direct to this part of the body in the trachea . . . in these tubes . . . so this is the difference . . . it isn't transported or carried around the body in the bloodstream like ours is. . . . It goes direct to the part of the body that needs it using the tubes or trachea.

This well illustrates the difficulty facing any teacher who tries to use words to convey her systematic understanding of a physical process. What the teacher said in the previous lesson has become 'It's got a lot of tubes in its body'. The teacher first makes a purely stylistic paraphrase into 'the

insect has tubes running through its body'; such priority
seems strange when the pupil has clearly no organized
recollection of the process taught. The teacher then (very
skilfully) makes explicit the function of the trachea by
contrast with human processes. It is possible that the
pupil if questioned would have remembered some of this.
But it would not be clear whether the teacher's language
meant to him the structure and sequence which it meant to
her. He might say the words, and yet still mean 'a lot of
tubes'. It will only be through some reference from
language towards what it represents – or towards some
more direct means of representation, such as pictures or
microscope slides – that the teacher will be able to ensure
that she is *handing over the meaning as well as the words*.

Some teachers behave as if they were confusing the
teaching of language forms with teaching their meaning.
In Lesson F the teacher is able to communicate with one
boy through the language of his subject, chemistry:

P   Please sir, could you purify the acetone to get it back?
T   Well you can actually, yes ... by process of what?
P   Distillation.
T   By process of distillation. .... We used it before. ...

This grammar school pupil is unusual in his ability to
think like a chemist and to use the specialist language. (It
is worth noting, perhaps, that this sequence is unique
amongst those we have quoted in that it is pupil initiated;
perhaps the two characteristics are associated.) He and
his teacher communicate easily. One of his companions is
less successful. (The teacher is trying to draw from the
class the suggestion that acetone or carbon tetrachloride
might be used to dissolve chlorophyll.)

T   You've got the green stain on your trousers. .... Could
    anyone suggest an alternative way ... other than by using
    water ... to get this green stain off again?
P   Um ... you couldn't use shoe polish and then give them a
    good wash?
T   No, I wouldn't try that [laughs] ... er I wouldn't try that
    on my new suit anyway. ....

P   Er ... er ... I mean floor polish.
T   Floor polish?
P   Yes, rub it in hard and then give them a good wash.
T   Er when you've tried that way you'll have to let me know
     how it works [laughs].

The teacher failed to perceive what is patent in a transcription, that this pupil had reached the general idea of
using a solvent. Since he had neither the general term
'solvent' nor knowledge of a specific solvent which would
be appropriate, he cannot let the teacher know this.
Therefore the teacher rejects what was potentially a
highly relevant contribution, partly because throughout
the lesson he was limited to the language of the specialism,
and unaware of chemical concepts when they were not
couched in stylistically appropriate language.

In sharp contrast to this is a teacher who accepts a
manifestly inadequate definition because it is clear that
the child understands the word in its present context
(Lesson B; 1966; secondary modern).

T   I have written on the board this pair [i.e. the figures
     7, 8]. . . . Will you mark the point . . . which that pair . . .
     denotes? What do I mean by 'denotes'?
P   Where it is.
T   Where it is. Yes.

This teacher is not so wedded to his term 'denotes' as to
allow it to interpose between the child and the process he
is learning.

It is the teacher of Lesson G (1966; physics; comprehensive school) who makes the most consistent effort to use
language which will carry precise meaning to his pupils
without building a wall of formality between them. 'The
tin box only moves a tiny bit so the pointer has got to move
a big lot', and 'Why does the tin have crinkly edges?'
and 'It would be really squashed-in-like'. Some teachers
feel that this is a betrayal of standards, but this is probably
not justifiable. Although the reader cannot tell whether
'crinkly' means 'serrated' or 'corrugated' or something

else, this must have been clear enough in the lesson. Nor can the colloquial '–like' be objected to except upon grounds of social propriety. The language serves its purpose well: it directs the pupils' attention to the appropriate aspect of the apparatus, when the very unfamiliarity of technical terms might discourage attentiveness. If it is argued that pupils will later require a more specialized register at least for their written work, this may well be conceded. Yet this teacher, by encouraging pupils to talk about his subject matter in terms which they already possessed, was probably helping them more effectively towards this, than a teacher who threw his pupils in at the deep end of his own adult language. Because of an inadequate recording it is impossible to give any lengthy quotations of the kind of participation by the pupils which this teacher's informality made possible. Some impression of their contributions can, however, be gained from isolated questions such as: 'Please sir, if you go up a high mountain when you get near the top you can feel sick', and 'Sir, if you climbed a high height in a car, would the engine stop?' These are quite different from the contributions of any other class, even in the same school. It is easier to illustrate the teacher's style:

T This is almost the same as that one . . . a slightly different arrangement . . . cut in half . . . you see it? . . . little tin can . . . silver thing in the middle . . . silver thing with circles on it? . . . that's that tin can . . . tin can just like that one . . . all right . . . on a good day then what is going to happen to the shape of that? Is it going to go . . . down? . . . Do you know? . . . See what happens to the pointer. Well that pointer's got to be connected. . . .

It seems reasonable to assume that this teacher's unusual language, informal and yet exactly adjusted to the apparatus, is related to his pupils' equally unusual degree of active participation in the lesson. This is not, of course, to argue that pupils should not eventually be asked to write in a more formal way about this material, once they have mastered it.

In this section we have raised a number of questions about how a teacher's use of language may be affecting his pupils' learning. This has been sketchy for two reasons: the material only occasionally shows this relationship with any clarity; and as the interaction is between behaviour and its meaning it has been possible to offer little more than surmises which deserve further investigation by other means.

Teachers' Awareness of Language

This informal study has now been carried out with two groups of teachers acting as investigators. With both groups there was a marked change of attitude to the study when the analysis was made. Until that point the material had been in their eyes no more than recordings of ordinary lessons: the analysis, however, brought out implications which they had failed to perceive as observers of the lessons. And as they themselves were making the analysis, they did not resist these new perceptions, as they might have done had they been offered to them in lectures. Later they made further discoveries which had gone unnoticed in the first analysis: these came to light in group discussion. Thus, the study so far provides a basis for arguing (a) that some teachers fail to perceive the pedagogical implications of many of their own uses of language, and (b) that a descriptive study such as this provides a potential method of helping teachers to become more aware. Whether they are able to carry over this insight into their own work has not been shown, however.

It is perhaps of value to summarize from the preceding pages those aspects of language to which teachers' attention might usefully be directed.

(a) Teachers need a far more sophisticated insight into the implications of the language which they themselves use, especially the register which we have called the language of secondary education.

(b) Teachers should study 'the gulf' between teacher and pupil which is at once linguistic and conceptual. Can specialist terminology hinder learning?

(c) Some aspects of the role of language in learning should be stressed. How do children learn new concepts, and what part can terminology play in this?

(d) A study of closed and open questions would throw light on the problem of dealing with private misconceptions, and upon the value of discussion. What is the value of encouraging pupils to 'think aloud' at length? What importance should be given to insisting that pupils make explicit what they have learnt either outside school, or in non-verbal terms inside school?

(e) Teachers should learn how their own behaviour in the classroom may embody teaching objectives of which they are unaware. How does a pupil learn to be a learner? How do the teacher's control methods affect this?

(f) Teachers should be more aware of their own assumptions so that they make explicit to pupils the criteria by which their performance will be accepted or rejected.

The purposes of such study would be frankly pedagogical. Teachers would study examples of classroom interaction, and look through the language at the learning and teaching. The purposes would be quite other than those of theoretical linguistics as the subject is often taught in colleges and universities.

What is clear from this study – in so far as these teachers fairly represent their colleagues in other schools across the country – is that teachers would gain from a more sophisticated insight into the implications of their own use of language, and into the part that language can at best play in their pupils' learning. The present writer inclines to believe that, if such insights were made available to all secondary teachers, they would contribute dramatically to the effectiveness of teaching in secondary schools.

But to write as if this were all a matter of language alone is to distort it. This discussion has not been concerned with language only but with the human interplay of which it forms part. In effect those who have participated in it have been saying to themselves: 'If you talk in this way rather than that way, you will limit the way your pupils can participate in your lessons and therefore limit their learning.' So that what has been said about language is also about relationships in the classroom and the learning that goes on there. Finally we want our pupils to perceive the world as a place which is orderly but infinitely responsive to new ways of saying and doing things. We can best help them to reach this by making our classrooms places of the same kind.

References

Barber, C. L., 'Some measurable characteristics of modern scientific prose', in Behre, F. (ed.), *Contributions to English Syntax and Philology*, Gothenburgh U.P., 1962.

Bernstein, B. B., 'Social class and linguistic development: a theory of social learning', in Halsey, A. H., Floud, J., and Anderson, C. A. (eds.), *Economy, Education and Society*, Free Press of Glencoe, 1961.

Bernstein, B. B., 'A socio-linguistic approach to social learning', in Gould, J. (ed.), *Social Science Survey*, Penguin Books, 1965.

Bruner, J. S., *On Knowing*, Harvard U.P., 1962.

Flanders, N. A.: see Amidon, E. J., and Hough, J. B. (eds.), *Interaction Analysis: Theory, Research and Application*, Addison-Wesley, 1967.

Flower, F. D., *Language and Education*, Longmans, 1966.

Holt, J., *How Children Fail*, Pitman, 1964.

Holt, J., *How Children Learn*, Pitman, 1968.

Joos, M., *The Fine Clocks*, Mouton, 1962.

Rosen, H., 'The language of textbooks', in Britton, J. (ed.), *Talking and Writing*, Methuen, 1967.

For an introduction to Professor Bernstein's ideas see: Lawton, D., *Social Class, Language and Education*, Routledge & Kegan Paul, 1968.

Acknowledgements

I should like to record my indebtedness to the University of Leeds Institute of Education, since this paper describes work done in courses leading to Advanced Diplomas of that Institute. I should like to thank too the head teachers and their colleagues who allowed us to invade their classrooms with tape recorders, and the ten teachers and lecturers who worked with me in transcribing and studying the lessons: Mr G. Collins, Miss H. Corlett, Miss J. Ede, Mr R. S. Ellis, Miss D. Fawthrop, Mr A. C. Fraser, Mr E. R. Jenkins, Mr D. R. O. Paige, Mr J. W. Saunders and Miss M. H. Taylor.

Part Two

Talking to Learn

James Britton

We teach and teach and they learn and learn: if they didn't, we wouldn't. But of course the relation between their learning and our teaching isn't by any means a constant one. From any given bit of teaching some learn more than others: we teach some lessons when everybody seems to learn something, and other lessons when nobody seems to learn anything – at all events, not anything of what we are 'teaching'. As the syllabus grows longer we teach more – but do they learn more? And if we get three lessons a week when we ought to have five, presumably we teach more to the minute than we would otherwise: but again, do they learn any quicker? How *do* we judge how much is being learnt, in any case?

It's easy enough to test simple rote learning of course (from nonsense syllables through Kim's Game to the Thirty-Nine Articles), but this goes no way towards satisfying our idea of what learning and teaching *are*. We want children, as a result of our teaching, to *understand*; to be wise as well as well-informed, able to solve fresh problems rather than have learnt the answers to old ones; indeed, not only able to answer questions but also able to ask them. Information as to how well they're getting on in this kind of learning – even if we could spend half our time devising and setting and marking tests – would be terribly hard to come by.

With considerations of this sort in mind, it seems useful to take time off to think about learning, look for examples of it in progress, forgetting teaching altogether for the moment. If the teacher could be more certain what learning looked like, in some at least of its many guises, he might find it easier to 'monitor' his own teaching.

Since learning doesn't take place to numbers, however,

and will probably sometimes take place in a very disorderly fashion, it is impossible to set it out, marshalled and docketed like the exhibits in a museum. Glimpses of it are to be found, first, in what people say to each other.

The first example presents a group of five sixteen-year-old girls talking about their homes. They come from the leavers' class in a comprehensive school, and the discussion arose as part of work on the B.B.C. Schools Radio programme, 'Speak'. There is no adult present.* The transcript cannot show all that was said because every now and then snatches of general – or dual or triple – talk break out, and perhaps only a word or two emerges. But it is as faithful as I can make it. Since such a conversation represents people acting upon each other, I have tried to keep the speakers clear in the record by giving each an identifying letter. Words in brackets are what emerges from general talk or else unidentified interruptions – though as we shall see the term 'interruption' does not do justice to the supportive tone that most of the interpolations carry. Speakers B and D are West Indian girls, the remainder – as their speech indicates on the tape itself – are Londoners.

A This is always happening in our house. (Really?) My dad brings home things and . . . you know, my mum comes along and she says, Right, this is no good, we'll get rid of this, we'll get rid of that, what's this doing here, we don't need this . . .

B No, and doesn't ask first . . .

C Load of old junk . . . throw it out!

A You can't blame her really . . .

B Yes, I know, but they have some things that you might think are old junk as well . . . that could be taking up space, you know . . .

A Like old exercise books . . .

C Yes, you wouldn't throw *those* away for anything . . .

*The 'starter' for the discussion was an extract from a short story, *Now I Lay Me*, by Ernest Hemingway. The girls followed the suggestion for talk in the teachers' notes on the passage. Part of their discussion was subsequently used in the broadcast programme called 'Parents'.

B I mean . . . I put certain things down in one place where I
know they are and suddenly my mother comes and she says,
Come on, we haven't got room for that . . . (Yes, . . . or she
says . . .) and I say, Well, where *can* I put it? Or she throws
it away and says, Oh! did you want it? [Laughter]

C Sorry, but it was cluttering up the room . . . you might as
well have thrown it away . . . it's no good.

A It's always causing rows in our family. . . . My brother says,
Where's my cricket set?

D I think it happens in any family unit, actually.

B I think it's just thoughtlessness for the other person . . . they
probably think because you're younger, what you do have to
put away is not worthwhile but as they're older people . . .
you know . . . they . . .

A Have you ever . . . you know . . . sort of . . . Mum's said to
you, like, Could you help me clear up? So you say, Yes,
O.K., and you put your brother's or sister's things away, and
then they come up and they say, Where's so and so? (Yeah
. . . Yes) But then you think to yourself, Well, it's annoying
to have . . . to have . . . to leave somebody's coat or something in the middle of the room . . . (Yes . . . Yes, I know . . .)
Do you know what I mean?

B And when they do complain, you feel as if you haven't done
your job, but then you say, Well, I did pack it away, didn't
I? . . . You know . . . what are they complaining about?

D It's annoying as well. . . .

E I do the same . . . I mean if I find anything lying around . . .
if it's no good I just throw it away. . . .

A It might mean a lot. . . .

D I think in my family . . . I think my mother is the most con-
siderate . . . she'd ask rather than my father . . . my father
wouldn't.

A Well, I'm lucky . . . I've got a room of my own . . . so . . .

D I'd like a room of my own, but then again, you don't keep
everything in your room, do you? My dad or mother goes
in there and finds anything that she doesn't think is necessary . . . my mother would ask me first, but my dad . . .

B Well, frankly, my mother wouldn't touch anything in my
room, you know . . . she just doesn't. She feels I've put it
there for some purpose . . . but again, if I go into her bedroom . . . (Yeah . . . That annoys me. . . .) But say if I have a
day off from school . . . or when . . . or we've got some sort
of holiday and I see things around and I say, well, you know,

I'll give the place a good old clean, at least it'll help . . . and I put things neatly, it's all tidy . . . I wouldn't throw anything out, because I'm not sure whether she wants it or not . . . and then she comes home, she says, Where's this? where's that? . . . I feel awful. . . .

D And you feel that . . . um . . . she doesn't appreciate . . .

B . . . appreciate, you know . . . I even the other day moved her bedroom . . . er . . . (Furniture) . . . furniture around.

D I did that in my house . . .

B I did . . . I thought it looked awful where it was, you know.

A But I . . . what annoys me is my room . . . is my room. . . . If . . . if it's in a muddle I know where everything is . . . I like my room to be in a mess.

B But you see, we . . . I keep that as a sort of main bedroom, you know . . . (main room . . .) Yes, sometimes I don't even sleep in my room, it's so cold. . . .

C Ooh, crumbs!

B How do you feel on this subject, Pamela?

D [with a great guffaw] Negative!

C I always know where everything is in my room even if it is untidy, but my mother comes along and I can't find anything anywhere.

A I like it when you get to that age where your parents seem to realize that you're . . . you're going off on your own . . . (Yes . . . You're growing up . . .) . . . you've got your own life to lead, so you think, Right, we'll leave all her things, she can do what she likes with them. It's her time, she can do what she likes with her time.

B They start from a certain point, don't they?

E Well, I don't think they always do that. . . . They try to remember that you're growing up and then they forget.

D Yes . . . they try to protect you. . . .

E They're treating you like children and telling you where to put things. . . .

C . . . going round tidying up after you.

E You know, I usually arrange my bedroom as I want it and then my mum comes along, Oh, you'll catch a draught there . . . it's no good, you don't want it that way . . . (Yes. Yes.) . . . and they move it around you know.

A I feel like the bed by the window, but they say no . . . I like to look out you know . . . see what's going on.

B I like it as well, you know . . . I like the head of my bed to be right by the window, you know, and my mother comes along and she says, Where's the North Pole? you know, Where's north? . . . all this business. . . . What's north got to do with it, you know . . . north and south . . . you know, you should have your head facing such-and-such. . . . Oo, I think it's just fuss, fuss . . . I don't like it at all.

D They're trying to do their best to protect us but sometimes they do overdo it.

B And things like if I don't draw my curtains when I go to bed . . . well, I like to see a half light streaming in, you know.

Already, it seems, the reader will be asking questions. How much of this talk is simply 'for the record' – an effect of the presence of the microphone? Does any individual girl in fact represent ideas that she really subscribes to? Or is each of them merely offering common currency, the small change of talk among their elders? Alternatively, in a different image, are they doing more than taking a nice warm dip together in comfortable beliefs that they all hold, have all talked about often enough before? Is anything happening to anybody in this talk – is anybody changing, or laying herself open to change?

Before pursuing these questions, let us look at a very different example of talk. A class of third-year girls (in their second year of Latin) was set the task of translating English sentences into Latin. They worked in groups of three, and here is a brief record of one trio:

A [reading] 'All the pupils are not praised by the teacher.'

B Where is it? [Laughter]

C All the pupils are not . . . third . . . (Yes) Are . . .

B Are not praised. . . .([Several voices] No.)

C Are not being praised. . . .

A Er . . . to praise . . .

C Um . . . *antur.*

A So it's . . .

B Yes, so its . . . um . . . *laudantur.* [Writing] *Laud-ant-ur.*

A All right. So we've got that out of the way.

B We've got to make sure whether it's singular or plural. . . .

A Mm. They are . . .

B They . . .

A Yes, so it's right. Um . . . now the subject (Pupils) . . . which
is er . . .

B *Discipulus.*

C *Discipuli* . . .

B *Discipuli*, yes, because it's plural.

C All the . . . all the . . .

B All the – what's 'all'?

C Mm . . . don't know, is there a word for it?

A Yes, *cuncti.*

C So it'll be *cuncti discipuli.*

B Or *omnis* . . . which shall we use?

A *Cuncti.*

C *Cuncti discipuli.*

B Mm . . . by the teachers . . .

A By the teachers . . . so it's ablative. . . . So it's. . . . Yes, so it's
magis. . . . [Laughter]

C Um . . . *magi* . . . um . . .

A You ought to know that.

C Yes, I know – ablative. . . . *Magistra.*

B I've got . . .

A Now, what does it read?

B *Cuncti discipuli magistra non laudantur . . . laudantur.*
[Laughter] Yes – they are!

C Oh! you've got to have . . . that . . . shouldn't you?

B Oh . . . um . . . *A magistra.*

A Why?

C Yes . . . *A magistra*, I think.

B *Cuncti discipuli a magistra laudabantur.* . . .

A *Laudantur* . . . [reading] 'Heavy burdens will not . . . will
be carried by the sad slaves.' . . . Heavy.

B *Gravis.*

C *Gravis.*

A *Onerus.*

C It's a passive verb.

B I know, but you've got the subject is 'heavy burdens' . . .
no, slaves are the subject, so slaves would be . . . er . . .
servis. Sad . . . *tristis . . . tris . . . tristes.*

A *Tristis . . . tristes . . . tristes* . . .

B *Servis* . . .

C Um . . . accusative, isn't it?

A No, it's ablative. Sad. . . . The verb will be 'will be carried'.

C The subject is . . .

B *Portatur* . . .
A *Portabuntur*. . . . Will be carried by the sad slaves. . . .
B *A servis . . . servi* . . .
C No, you should . . . um . . . heavy burdens is the subject, because that's what it's having done to it, you see.
B I know, but couldn't we . . .
C Burdens is having the thing done to it.
A Yes, so you should start with the subject.
C Which is heavy burdens.
A *Onerus . . . onera . . . grava . . . gravia*. Um – by the sad slaves, for the last time . . .

The contrast between the two examples is evident enough, but they are not offered in order that one should be accepted and the other rejected. Their differences are of concern, but what is more important is first to consider each as an example of talking to solve problems, talking to learn. The problems facing the third-form girls were highly specific: should it be *laudatur* or *laudantur*, for example. They were able to commit themselves quickly, and their solutions, like the lights in a crossword puzzle, would before very long be proved right or wrong. To reach such solutions, however, they had to operate general principles, a kind of modified code based on the generative laws of the Latin language. Thus behind the problem of *laudantur* lay that of using the passive in Latin.

To a beginner, one might say, the use of the passive in Latin has many pitfalls: and in any situation full of pitfalls, three watchdogs are better than one. To that interpretation of the situation, however, at least three things must be added. First, the girl least adept at manipulating the passive in Latin is likely to learn to do it better by working with those more adept. Secondly, even the girl who is most adept at handling the passive in Latin is likely to improve her understanding of the principles involved under challenge of being asked to *explain* what so far she has accepted as 'obvious' or 'inevitable'. (As teachers we are familiar with that form of the wisdom of babes and sucklings that consists in asking the 'too simple' question.) And thirdly, one can conceive of a situation in which the application of general principles presented a novel difficulty that none of the group could solve at first, but which they *solved jointly* by talking their way through it.

But what is to be said about the first example – the talk about rooms and families by the sixteen-year-olds? Clearly they commit themselves to nothing that can readily be proved right or wrong. They are not arguing: no one seems particularly concerned to prove anybody else wrong nor is anyone put in the position of having to prove herself right. And as for the speed of the operation, the dominant impression from the extract must be that if anything happens at all it will achieve itself in its own good time. If we ask, are the speakers merely supporting each other in already accepted familiar opinions (whether genuinely held or assumed, and whether prejudices or well-grounded opinions), we shall probably find it impossible to arrive at a satisfactory answer for the very reason already given – that the pace is leisurely and we need to see it cover a longer span.

That is therefore what I propose to do. But first something may be said on the basis of the extract already quoted. It seems fair to comment that the speakers do appear to be speaking their own minds: the consensus appears to be a consensus of their own views, not very much affected by the knowledge that adults may later be listening to what they say. There is a mixture here: some of the statements are complaints against their parents, invidious comparisons – things they might voice to their parents in anger, or even in cold blood, but not in the genial cum tolerant cum affectionate cum condescending tones of this talk; others seem to pose an adult view – or perhaps, rather, move towards such a view. Again, there are some observations that are clearly made from their own experience and not that of their parents – as, for example, when the 'good girl', by tidying up for her mother, gets in wrong with her brothers and sisters. In fact, if one were to hazard a formulation of what is beginning to happen in this extract, it might be to say that the group is gently probing to see how far it can go towards reconciling a daughter's viewpoint with that of a parent.

One direct outcome of a few minutes' talk by the third formers was a sentence in Latin: the sixteen-year-olds have nothing remotely like it, have in fact here no practical outcome directing their efforts. What they achieve in the way of learning – if they achieve anything at all – will have to be measured against some other yardstick. Here then the tape continues – back among the bed-rooms:

B And things like if I don't draw my curtains when I go to bed . . . well, I like to see a half light streaming in you know.

D The thing is, with my bedroom, I haven't . . . can't have a view really, 'cos it adjoins the bathroom, you see, and . . .

B Oh, I know.

C I have to share mine with my sister.

B You share with your sister?

C Yeah.

E I've got my own now but it's rather small. . . .

A I think it's a shame though . . .

C A box-room, wasn't it?

E More or less . . . yes.

A I think it's a shame when you live in a flat or a small house and your parents want the best for you and they try to get you a room on your own. My mum often goes round saying, Oh, if I had a big house, I'd have a music room and a reading room . . .

B Yeah, all different rooms.

A They really want the best for you, you know . . . you're pleased at that . . . but the trouble is they feel as though they've not done all they could. (Yeah).

B And you don't want them to feel that way, do you? (No) Because you know, you can only . . .

E The thing I like, you know, is when you come in in the evenings and there's only one room, one main living-room to go to . . . and you have to get on with everyone, so you talk and you say what's happened to you during the day and . . . you know . . . it's good to get on . . . (Yes. Mm)

A It's also nice to have somewhere to get away from all the time. (Yes. . . . Yes, I think so) Because . . . I mean . . . at this stage, parents can be very annoying . . . and ruin you. . . . They've got different ideas. I mean . . . you know . . . you might . . . they might say something, you can answer them back . . . and to them, just to answer them is being cheeky or impudent. (Yes) They don't realize you're just . . . because you're talking to them as if they were a friend . . . how I think it should be . . . (Yeah. Yeah) . . . they don't remember that, and they . . . sort of . . . you know . . . sort of think, You're my daughter and so . . . you know . . . (Yeah)

D . . . especially if I wanted to start a discussion on anything . . . music perhaps . . . my father would say, Oh, that . . . symphonies and so forth are rubbish . . . I mean, go on as if he was telling me off . . . I'm only trying to start a discussion . . . about music, and that. . . .

B Just a general argument. I think the trouble is, they're so used to putting their point and making it. . . . Well, that's that and it's right . . . that when they get somebody that comes along and puts a different point to them . . . makes a different point to the matter . . . it's different . . . they can't understand it, you know.

A I think that's a good thing . . .

B And with my mother . . .

E You do?

A Yes. To have a row is good . . . it gets it out of your system. (Yes. I think so)

B To have a row is good, I think . . . Well, the trouble with me I never stop at one thing . . . I always want to prove I'm right.

E My parents bring up something else what happened a long time ago. (Yes. . . . Yeah)

D My father is always referring back . . . I remember when you were ever so little, you never used to talk to me like that . . . I said, I've grown up.

B You couldn't, could you? . . . But then again, in this book, there's another point, isn't there . . . I think this is the point . . that the child talks about praying and how many people it prays for . . . and then by the time it's finished, it's daylight you know. And then, near the end, it says, but then again there *are* only two people.

A Two main people . . .

B Two main people there, yeah. But then . . . so . . . I think this signifies that whatever might happen between you and your parents, no matter what . . . they are there . . . and it means something, you know, just that they're there, even.

E There are some people that'll go through things with you that are nice . . . you know . . . to do, but when it comes to you asking someone to do something that's not very nice . . . you know . . . you hate doing . . . (Yeah) . . . they're always there.

B Your parents, yeah.

E If you have a row with a friend that you like, you know . . . that you get on well with . . . there aren't many people you can talk about it to, 'cause usually you're in a circle of friends that you all know each other . . . but your parents are always there, you know.

A It's all right for some people . . . I mean, it's not too bad for me . . . but some people can't talk to their parents . . . and girls can't talk to them. (No) With normal people, you know . . . it's still this, a mother and child.

B Do you think it's because . . .

A It's the same as some teachers who still think that . . . you know . . . We're the teachers and we've got to teach you . . . you're just the children. . . . You know, they can't talk to each other as if they were sort of . . . on the same level.

D I don't think there's so much of that in our school though.

B No there isn't . . . I don't think there is at all . . .

At this point they spend a minute or two talking about school, about the need to learn how to put your own views and the difficulties of doing so. I am reluctant to cut the tape because one of the points I want to illustrate is the slow evolution that is one of the forms learning may take – and the need to give the process time. The *circularity* of much of the discussion will be clear. It moves on, certainly, with little hesitation and very little back-tracking: probably the only clear example of back-tracking – or a blind alley – in the whole tape is the exchange on page 84 where a consideration of some relationship between rooms and sleeping – put forward by B – is rejected by D's 'Negative!' But progress is a kind of spiral: thus A on page 89 drops a hint when she says, 'but the trouble is they feel as though they've not done all they could.' B takes it up and appears to be on the point of offering an explanation, but E interrupts with a point compelling enough to shift the course of the conversation. And the question of guilt – and its infectiousness in the home – does not return for some time.

To return to the tape for another extract or two – for, unfortunately, the record is too long to be given in full: B has firmly steered the talk back from school and related matters to the problems of the family. They talk about having to look after grandparents, with obvious implications about their own parents growing old, and this leads on to a pretty unanimous vote of confidence:

E I think that's part of growing up . . . that . . . um . . . to know what your parents have said to you all along . . . well, it's true. (. . . appreciate the fact . . .)

B Well, it's true, I can appreciate them more. To experience it in life and find out that it's true . . . you know . . . 'cause that's the best way . . . when you experience it.

D Yes, it's hard to believe it even though it is your parents telling you.

A You don't seem to believe your parents, do you, until it happens and then you can't believe it . . .

B No . . . until you find out . . . till you find out from yourself.

E I think round about now, you know, you start to realize . . . your parents do know much better than what you do.

B I mean, you might not admit it . . . ten to one you don't! (No) [Laughter]

They go on to elaborate this confidence in their parents' views, mainly in terms of views about boys and dating. Then A breaks into a new vein:

A When we used to live in . . . in Kennington . . . they used to walk . . . we used to walk across the bridge . . . you know, walk round London . . . used to be ever so happy and I can remember my parents walking along hand in hand . . . you know . . . giggling [Laughter] . . . and there's me in between, you know, looking up . . . and laughing our heads off we were . . . and I can remember that clearly as anything. It's one of the first things I remembered . . . you know, being very happy, just the three of us. Then the next thing I remember was me having to go away because my brother was born and he had pneumonia . . . and he came along and it was horrible . . . (Yes) [Laughter] . . . It split up the family . . . you know what I mean . . . I was really jealous.

E You were out of things . . .

A Yeah, I got really left out . . . and it's been a bit like that ever since. (I think that, like . . . Well, not only that . . .)

B I think parents begin to get out of touch with each other as husband and wife . . . slightly, I should think . . . I don't know . . . it all depends what the couple's life's like . . . er . . . when they start having children. You see it takes so much of their time . . . and it takes a certain place in their lives.

A The husband gets left out a lot, doesn't he? (Yeah . . . has a hard . . .) [Laughter] . . . No, you hear such a lot . . . when perhaps . . . when your dad come home in the evening and your mother will say, Just a minute I'm getting so and so's tea . . . Can you wait a bit? . . . you know, he's probably come home from work . . . (Yeah)

B Or, I've got my ironing . . . or, I've got to take the children to bed . . . and what not.

A Yeah, I think that's when they get . . .

D My dad comes home and he sits down and says, Will somebody get my slippers? and nobody moves, you know . . . Everyone's eating their dinner or staring at the television . . . He feels very neglected I think . . .

B Probably because he feels everything should be done to him, you know. (Yeah)

C He's the father . . . they should do everything for him . . .

D Probably been . . .

B Head of the house . . . as it were.

A . . . extra special attention . . . which I think is right, you know . . . I hope I remember that whenever I get married.

D He's the one that goes out to work . . . earns the money, as he says.

B But then again, you find some families who . . . don't take this attitude. They feel that . . . both should be the sort of . . . head . . . you know . . . leader.

A's recollection of her infancy encourages other girls to contribute theirs, and they give rise to such matters as parents who like to go out and those who like to stay in, the difficulties mothers have in getting out while the children are small, parents' attempts to educate their children, and so on. Then E, who has not yet contributed an early memory (and who has said nothing for a while) launches the group into the topic of our final extract:

E I think what you mainly remember is when . . . sort of . . . to your knowledge . . . your . . . the first time you see your mother and father having a row . . . Not a fight, but a row. (Yes) You always think . . . you always look at them to be . . . you know . . . you think, That's my mother and father . . . they're always so happy, you know, and I'm happy with them . . . but when you see them angry with each other . . . that just spoils everything. Sort of . . . you can't say, you know . . . then when you get older, you think, what if they got divorced . . . or had to separate . . . (Yes. Oh dear)

D It's on your memory all the while, isn't it?

E You think which one would you choose, and you can't . . . well, I can't . . . I couldn't choose between my mother and father.

A They seem to be one . . . they are one. (Yeah. They are) Parents, you don't think of them as two separate people.

D You don't split them up into mother and father . . .

A It's when they have rows that you realize they're two separate people . . . what could go wrong. (Yes)

D I don't want to take sides . . . I hate taking sides . . . because my mum will explain . . . she gets quite angry and she'll explain to me and tell me what happened . . . and then my dad will explain. Both the stories may be different . . . you know, the same sort of thing, but different . . . but I can see one of them isn't quite right and I can't say which one of them it is. (No)

C Have you ever had them say . . . whichever one it is . . . say you're always on his side? (Yes)

E I could never take sides, you know . . . if my father is . . . you know . . . shouting at my mother, I'd say, Don't shout at my mum like that! . . . and then my mother will start shouting at my dad and I'd say, Don't shout at my dad like that! . . . You know, I could never choose.

D I can't.

A I can remember the first row we ever had. It was . . . I think

... my brother and I were in the kitchen and my mum and dad were rowing and it was so bad ... I'd never seen a row like this before, and my mum just started crying her eyes out and my dad felt terribly guilty, he was dead silent. Then I started crying, my brother started crying ... it was hell for about half an hour, you know. We all split up, there was nothing of the family left. And then we all crept back in, giggling and saying, Oh, I am sorry, you know.

D Yes, that's the best part ...

B Well, frankly when my parents ... when they do have rows, you know, I ... er ... always saw both sides, because there was something in each ... one's explanation that ... that meant something. (Yes)

D You know, because each one's explanation was different, wasn't it?

B Yeah, and there was something right in each one. ... So I just couldn't realize why on earth they did have the row in the first place, because you ... you both have perfectly good reasons but they just don't fit in.

D Sometimes they don't realize how upsetting it can be to the child. The child sometimes doesn't want to show they're upset in front of the parents, do they?

B Yeah.

C Sometimes it's something silly and the child could see it's silly and wondering why they're rowing over it 'cause they wouldn't think of anyone rowing over it ... it's just silly.

A Yes, it's funny isn't it, children don't row so much as adults.

D Really? [Laughter] My brother and I, we row.

C My sister and I are terrible ...

D I think that happens to all families, doesn't it, when they've got brothers and sisters ...

E Yes, but now I think you get most rows because they're *over* you, you know. (Yes. ... Terrible) And you think you're the object of this row ... and you think, Ooh!

B You're always getting the blame for everything.

D ... and you're not really ... can't stick up for yourself.

B This is why sometimes ... sort of lose contact with each other ... because you sort of come between them in a way ... you know.

There it is then: the whole conversation lasted about thirty minutes, and of that I have given you some seventeen minutes' worth, extracting first from the beginning and lastly from very near the end.

The language remains 'expressive' throughout, in the sense that it is relaxed, self-presenting, self-revealing, addressed to a few intimate companions; in the sense that it moves easily from general comment to narration of particular experiences and back again; and in the special sense that in making comments the speakers do not aim at accurate, explicit reference (as one might in an argument or in a sociological report) and in relating experiences they do not aim at a polished performance (as a raconteur or a novelist would). I make this sketchy analysis here in the hope of returning to it later.

In their comments and their narration, the speakers offer their own evaluations of the behaviour they talk about: on the whole their individual evaluations agree with each other. Some differences come to light (as when A feels that adults quarrel more than children) and here it may well be that an individual will revise her evaluation – and of course there may be modifications made also to unspoken evaluations. But in general it is a sanctioning process that goes on: each enjoys the valuable social satisfaction of finding her evaluations sanctioned by her fellows.

I would want to call this in itself educative – might, by a sophistry, see it as 'learning that you need not un-learn'. But more needs to be said.

As the talk rolls on, we see as it were elements of the family situation laid out for inspection. They are not precise elements like 'subject' and 'passive' and 'third person singular', which when properly inspected and handled may come together as a Latin sentence. But they are there: parents are provided with a history – seen as young couples, with no children, free to go out; and as people with a future, old and needing help from those who now need them; and as separate people with separate likes and dislikes, though they usually feature in our minds as one; and as human beings capable equally of wise control and rows over silly nothings. Laid out also are the bits of the family jigsaw itself: father, the one who goes out to work; mother, the one who tidies – and is perhaps equally 'the leader'; brothers and sisters; grand-parents, the not-to-be-neglected. And the various ties that link the pieces in various ways together: love, happiness, protection, anger, guilt.

I am particularly interested in E's last contribution and will try now to explain why. Quarrelling had come into the conversation early on – but then simply as a good way of clearing the air: guilt had been hinted at, as has already been observed. E's behaviour might suggest – though nothing can be said for certain – the gestation of an idea. Silent for some minutes, she then produces, rather belatedly, her contribution to the 'I remember' series: and when it comes it breaks defences that none of the group has yet dared to breach – and goes the whole way. We see her recoiling from the guilt involved in choosing one parent to reject the other, and finally – forcing the conversation back to make her last point – confronting the guilt of being the cause of all the quarrelling. Doubtless she could not say so, yet she seems to know – with us – that, of all the emotions that bind a family together, feeling guilty about each other is the most treacherous. E, if I am right about her, would indicate that there is here more than the laying out of the elements of the problem: something is done with them. There is a spiral movement in all that 'circularity'.

In talk of this kind trivialities may break in at any moment (though it is never easy to be sure what is trivial in somebody else's concern): it does seem, how-ever, that as this conversation moves on it grows in its power to penetrate a topic and resist the trivial distractions. At its most coherent points it takes on the appearance of a *group effort at understanding*, and these coherent passages are more frequent in the later phases than in the earlier. There will be other virtues in argument and the clash of opinions: the mutually supportive roles these speakers play make it possible for them, I believe, to exert a group effort at understanding – enable them, that is, to arrive at conclusions they could not have reached alone and without that support.

If this is learning, it might be argued, then learning must be a very common phenomenon. No one would wish to dispute that: what I would argue is that a mode of learning so frequently practised ought to make more of a contribution to learning in school than, by and large, it is able to do as we organize things at the moment. And if teachers in fact came to the conclusion that it was no concern of the school to foster a better understanding among members of the family, their attention should still be drawn to this talk as exemplifying a means of learning that could be useful in other areas.

I think the reader will agree that those five girls showed considerable skill in the art of expressive speech. If expressive speech is a means of learning, they have at their disposal a pretty effective instrument. But of course the skill is something they had to *learn* – a fact that may not readily be realized since it is only the children of linguistically restricted homes that have not substantially learnt it before ever they come to school. I would hazard a guess that at least some of those five had in fact learnt it in school rather than at home.

Perhaps I can best put over the point I am trying to make by comparing the performance of those girls with that of two others. They are also school leavers, from a different school; they are discussing the same sort of themes. In this case there is a teacher present and though she is not saying much, the girls address their remarks mainly to her. Notice how little they generalize – how in fact when they embark on a generalization they seem very quickly to be drawn into particulars – and are likely to stay there long enough for the general statement to be forgotten. Thus it is difficult for one generalization to be built upon another. We may certainly draw general inferences from their particulars, but the speakers themselves do so rarely, and then perhaps incompletely.

A N . . . now, my boy-friend Tom, you know . . . now, if I go
home and talk to my dad about him like . . . if I'm in the shop
and something happens . . . it's funny or . . . see, I walked in
the shop and he was piling up some ba . . . little pears, see . . .
and I walked in and I must have slammed the door . . . I
didn't mean to . . . they all fell down, see, so he said, That's
the third time I've done that . . . so I did it . . . so I stacked
them all up you know . . . and they fell down when I did it,
so we both done it . . . and we got it all up . . . and I went
home to tell my dad, you know . . . My mum said . . . er . . .
Oh, that's all we hear about is him, we don't hear about anything else. And I don't talk about him all that much . . . but
that particular time it's . . . you know . . . it was really funny
the way he did it, you know . . . they all fell down, sort of
thing.

B I mean, it's only natural to talk about your boy-friend, init?
You'd think your parents would be interested, wouldn't
you? My dad . . . he says . . . er . . . he says to me, I don't
care . . . you know, sort of think, like that you know . . . My
mum's all interested, you know . . .

T It's hard though . . . isn't it . . . hard for parents to be int . . .
sort of interested in the proper way in boy-friends and girl-
friends . . . 'cause aren't they bound to feel a bit sort of
jealous of you . . . because you're their babies – going off,
you know, into the world.

A Mary's mum won't let her join a . . . what is it again?

B No, well . . . you see . . .

A A youth club, see . . . Now, we can . . . we were going to
join . . . [Laughter from B] . . . last Friday. Now I said to my
mum last night, Mum, I'll be going out Friday with Mary
. . . on Saturday. Where are you going? So I said, I'm going
. . . um . . . to join a youth club . . . said, Where is it? I said
. . . um . . . I think it's South Borough . . . isn't it?

B No . . .

A I said South Borough . . . I don't know where it was.

B It's Smith Street . . . it's only up the road . . .

A Oh, Smith Street . . . anyway, so I says . . . um . . . We're
going to join it, you know, and she says . . . umm . . Oh all
right then, you know . . . and she don't, like . . .

B . . . interested . . .

A . . . kind of ask you, you know, like . . . now . . . um . . .
Monday I usually go round Tom's to help him sometimes

you know with the shop because I ... he serves and I give the Green Shield stamps out ... and ... um ... anyway she ... um ... I usually go in there Fri ... Mondays and Sundays to help him sometimes ... anyway I goes down there Friday, and I gets back at seven o' clock ... that's when the shop shuts, and we went out. Anyway, when I got back about nine o'clock I said to Tom, I'm going back now ... said I don't fancy ... I wasn't all ... I didn't feel all that ... good ... good, you know. Anyway, so I went home and I ... when I'm not feeling well I go all quiet, you know ...

B ... sulky ...

A Anyway, so I'm just sitting there watching telly ... she said, What's the matter? Now if I have a row with Mary we usually make it up the next day, didn't we?

B We come to school ... say something like, Hi-ya, girl!

A Yeah. But then ... um ... she say to me, Oh you had a row with so and so so and so, you know ... and she'll keep on and on and on at me, you know, till I do ...

B 'Stead of trying to cheer you up, sort of thing ...

A Yeah, she'll keep on and on so in the end I just walked out. I just went out for a walk, you know ... I thought, can't I keep something to myself? You know ... the things I don't want to tell her I don't, you know ... I don't go home and tell her things that ... er ... I want to do like an ordinary child does ... I keep them to myself ... or tell my dad ...

B I do that sometimes. ... Do you think parents ... like they all make out if you sit indoors, you know ... nothing to do ... and they always saying, Why don't you go out, you know, or do something, you know, and when you find something to do like join a youth club or go a pictures with your mates ... they won't let you go ... it's silly, don't you think, though ...

T Well, I suppose parents get into just as much muddle as children do, in a way.

One of the inferences that might be drawn is that made by some of the teachers from that school: they believed that to help the girls to 'get somewhere' in their talk was one of the most generally helpful things they could do for them – something that would assist their work in all parts of the curriculum.

What does help mean in this case? First, of course, it means providing opportunity and an atmosphere of confidence and encouragement: that this was being done is clear from the tape. Secondly, it means entering into the talk at the right moment and in the right way. A tentative generalization offered opportunely in the give and take of conversation is obviously more helpful than any string of generalizations could be, spoken to a silent class. Such a contribution or, at a later stage, the question that invited the speaker herself to generalize – these would be life-lines to cling to when the whirlpool of particularities threatened to suck her down!

The struggle to organize their thoughts and feelings, to come up with words that would shape an understanding – the struggle to rise above the limitations of their language – can be sharply felt at times when reading the record:

B You know why that is . . . 'cause . . . 'cause when . . . when my brother and I was young you know, like, he used to hit us ever such a lot, you know . . . but when we . . . 'Cause he used to hit us so much my mum threatened to go to the police one day, you know . . . and ever since that day he's never touched us, you know . . . and I think . . . and he never used to show us any attention . . . you know, when your mum and your dad sit down and sort of read to you and try to teach you things . . . and all things like that, you know . . . and sums and that . . . he wouldn't do nothing like that . . . and my mum used to say to him that he won't get on with them when they get older if you don't take no attention to them . . . and he never took no attention to us at all . . . and I suppose that's why, init really? . . . and it just won't work out now 'cause he's left it too late, hasn't he? you know what I mean?

A final comment – though not one to be too serious about: at the end of this conversation they had come up with no better solution to their problems than the one they started with – a solution as particular as it was impractical:

A . . . my dad should marry her mum . . . and your dad should
   marry my mum and . . .
B . . . we both go and live with our mum and her dad, and let
   our other mum and dad get on together . . .

On the morning after they had finished taking their
C.S.E. examinations, four boys were talking to their
English teacher – and part of that conversation is the
next example. She asks them what they thought of their
fifth year at school: one boy (B in the transcript) states
his views: 'I mean, like, if you can get the same job the
year before – the same job as what you're going for if you
stay on at school a year there's not much point in staying
on, is there?' The teacher asks, 'Then what do you think
education is for – to get you jobs?' And so the topic of
education is taken up. It rapidly turns into argument. A
thinks you have to be educated 'so that you can go out and
take over from the older generation that are getting old and
take on civilization and put it forward, like'. His argument
is based, mainly, on the necessity of *invention*. C is in
favour of education 'so that you know what you're on
about'. (Someone refers to him as a motor-bike addict,
and he is certainly knowledgeable about cars.) B declares
his respect for education because it 'makes you a better
citizen', but apart from indicating that being educated
saves you from taking up crime he does not say what he
means by being a good citizen. Being mad on cars he has
picked up a great deal of know-how with regard to them –
by watching and having a go – and he values this sort
of knowledge, which seems to him to have nothing to
do with education. D sides with B on the whole, and
particularly opposes A on the grounds that the ability to
invent things comes from experience and not from
education.

The teacher is occasionally drawn into the ding-dong,
but more often comes in as a kind of chairman – trying
to get a sharper definition ('Well, what do you mean by
that?'), or to untangle particular knots ('Yes, well, what's
the other counter to C's argument?'), or to broaden the

perspective ('You're still seeing it in terms of jobs'), or occasionally to sum up the position reached.

The conversation lasted about forty minutes: what follows is a record of the last six minutes or so:

T This education you're talking about you know . . . it's just the acquiring of skills. Don't you see education as doing anything else?

A Educating.

T I mean, what about all the other subjects? Supposing . . .

B It broadens your mind . . .

T Supposing somebody was an absolutely superb mechanic . . .

B Yes?

C Yes?

T I don't know how you would assess that somebody was superb as a mechanic . . . but there was absolutely nothing that defeated him, and he could turn his mechanical skill to any vehicle – in fact any kind of machine. . . . One would have to admit that he was in that respect an educated man . . .

C No, you wouldn't.

T You wouldn't? Oh! I see . . .

C You wouldn't have to admit that he was educated, it's just that he's . . . gone into a job as an apprentice . . .

D He's just a craftsman.

C . . . and he's gone up in his job until he's top mechanic. He knows what he's doing. Same as you in your job. You know what you're doing, didn't you? Half the time!

D He's a craftsman, ain't he?

C As my . . .

A But he had to learn it. He just didn't get it like that.

B Listen, listen. . . . He says you've got to be educated to come out and learn a job, right? Learn a trade, right?

A You can't go out right dim?

B All right then, listen . . .

C My dad's a dumkopf – but he know's what he's on about.

B My dad came out of school. He left at fourteen, right?

A Yes.

B He went in the print. He jacked that in 'cos he didn't know nothing, he wasn't educated . . . he admits it . . . but then he went into an apprenticeship for plastering. Six years apprenticeship, right? Now he left school at fourteen.

A Yes . . . so he's six years . . . he had to learn about it first . . .

B I know, but you don't have to be educated to learn about it.

A I know – in special subjects you don't.

B You say you've got to be educated to do things though.

A You have got to be educated to do some things.

C Look, my dad can't tell mutton from . . . my dad, he's as
   dumb as me when it comes to maths. In fact he's dumber
   than me – he's dumber than me at English. Yet look at the
   job he's got. He's working in the print. He's worked as a
   barber. He rides motor-bikes, right? He used to do that as
   a job. He used to be a chauffeur. Now you can't tell me that
   to go out and get on a motor-bike and ride it and to drive a
   car, you've got to be educated.

D Eh – so you've got to be educated. Now listen to this. My
   old man, right? . . . he hardly went to school from about he
   was twelve, right? Because he was evacuated in the war,
   right? And he started off as a job, you know like, as a welder.
   He started off as a welder and then he went into lorry-
   driving, right? Long distance. Now he's a manager. Where'd
   he get the education from that?

A Yes, but you say, look, when these people invented these
   things . . . they weren't . . . they weren't . . . they weren't as
   . . . like us, were they? . . . years ago. . . . They weren't like
   us. They were rich people mainly . . . who'd been to school
   because their people . . . their parents had sent them to
   school . . . who invented all these things?

B People . . .

A And they were educated.

C They had to pay to go to school.

A And during the war, people who invented things had been to
   school.

B People during the war . . .

D No, it wasn't . . .

A Near enough all . . .

D People then . . . to do experiments . . .

B No . . . 'cause all they had is the roof over their heads . . .
   which wasn't too safe.

C We're not talking about during the war . . . we're talking
   about the first aeroplanes and cars and that. . . . The blokes
   that invented them . . . in those days when they were invented . . . to go to school your mother and father had to pay
   enormous sums of money . . .

B Not necessarily . . .

C . . . and most of them went to school.

B And what happened if you went to orphans' school?

A And that proves your point that you've got to be educated.

B No, it doesn't though . . .

C Yes.

A None of us people, right low down in the working class . . . they never invented hardly anything, did they? It was rich people – because they'd been to school.

D So they went to school – so they went to school. They're not going to learn about engines and that because they hadn't been invented. . . . They invented them when they left school.

A That's what I mean, and . . . yes, they was educated, wasn't they?

D What for? They hadn't got to be educated about engines.

C They had to work out the compression ratios, gear ratios, everything like that. You can't do that without maths, can you?

B A one . . . a one-cylinder engine . . . the compression ratio is slightly easy to work out.

C Yes, but a little kid of four couldn't do it, could he?

B I know . . . he hasn't got the mental ability.

C No – neither have I. I couldn't work out the compression ratio.

B You haven't got the mental ability of a kid of four . . .

C I know . . . well, then . . .

B You couldn't . . .

C You can laugh . . .

The argument is good tempered in a bantering way, but gets quite heated as it goes on, and makes a fairly noisy tape. The sharp retort, the flat contradiction, rejection both by counter-statement and by abuse, a steam-rollering use of repetition, and occasional fierce competition to be heard – all these features set up a very different situation from the mutually supportive talk in our first example. Above all the speakers set up what is tantamount to a demand on each other to be *more explicit* – and the teacher does so deliberately. To comply would require a move from expressive speech to a more *referential* mode, from speech that tells us a good deal about the speaker –

his feelings about teachers, about the topic under discussion and about his particular, current contribution to it – to speech that designates more accurately, refers more specifically.

Look however at the following exchange taken from this argument:

B   As I've said before . . .
C   'It makes you a better citizen!'
B   Well it does.
T   Well, what do you mean by that?
B   Well, if you've been educated you appreciate things more, don't you? Right . . . so if you see someone's nice new shiny car, you won't go up with a dirty great big knife and go crr . . . crr . . . down the side.

C's mocking quotation of what B has said several times before might suggest that in C's opinion they don't get much further by merely repeating that formula: he doesn't say so, but rejects B's contribution by a mild form of abuse. The teacher does ask B to explain, to be more explicit. His reply, 'you appreciate things more', is clearly not more but less explicit – since one who appreciates things more might presumably make a better lover, a better husband, a better artist, a better tenant – as well as a better citizen. However, B's example then indicates that it was a better citizen he had in mind – if we accept his assumption that appreciating cars more is what makes you respect another man's property. In exemplifying what he means he is in a sense being explicit, but only in a sense: it is not the *idea* of 'being a better citizen' that is made explicit, only the example – the idea, the generalization, is implicit in the example, not explicit.

It does seem that these four boys are linguistically more advanced than the two girls in the preceding example: in response to the demands of the topic, and of the activity they are engaged in (argument), they do produce a considerable number of general statements. Yet repeatedly, at just the point when a more explicit generalization is demanded, they respond with a particular statement, some kind of exemplification. When, for example, A makes his claim that you need to be educated 'so that you can go out and take over from the older generation . . . and take on civilization and put it forward', he gives, as examples of people having done this, the invention of aeroplanes and 'getting to the moon'. He is then taken up by B *at the level of the examples*: 'Anyone can make aeroplanes that have got the plans and all that in front of him.' It is by a series of similar steps – interactions at the level of example – that the argument finally breaks down in the long extract printed here.

In the course of the discussion as a whole, quite a few of the ideas needed to explain what education is and what it does are referred to. For example:

'That's instinct, isn't it? That's just curiosity – what you were born with.' (A)
'When we get older, like, we discover about things about us.' (D)
'mental ability' . . . (B)
'been brought up that way . . .' (A)
'apprenticeship . . .' (B)
'you need experience . . . if you worked by 'em and worked with 'em you could . . .' [build an aeroplane] (D)
'you have to learn by doing it yourself' . . . (C)
'You'd stand there and you'd watch and you'd learn. That's education – learning.' (A) 'No, no – you learn yourself.' (D)

Some of the useful elements of the topic are thus 'laid out'. But, in the heat of the argument, very little is done with them and certainly they are not manifestly put together to arrive at any solution, any resolution of the conflicting opinions.

There is also, as might be expected, a wealth of exemplification: Boeing 707s, space flight, the teacher's car, primitive tribes, cave-men, the Mafia, munition workers – all these and many other things are brought in to serve the speakers' arguments. They fail to do so, as we have seen. To realize what view of education is implied by another speaker's example means envisaging *alternative possibilities* to the view you hold yourself: and these boys seem able to do this only fleetingly and partially. They make very general statements on the one hand and give concrete particulars on the other: the one is too general to provide a testable hypothesis and the other so particular as to constitute in itself no hypothesis at all. The intermediate generalizations needed to bridge the gap are something they can neither supply for their own statements nor derive from other people's.

I have quoted B's early remark: 'I mean, like, if you can get the same job the year before . . . there's not much point in staying on, is there?' To a varying extent all the speakers make use of such expressions as, 'I mean', 'like', 'sort of', 'you know' and the question tag after a state- ment – 'is there?', 'would he?', 'don't you?' and so on; and they all at some time use the term 'right' in a some- what similar fashion. Expressions of this kind have been called (by Professor Basil Bernstein) expressions of 'sympathetic circularity'. They constitute an appeal to the opinions and sentiments held in common by the group. 'I mean', 'like', 'sort of' and 'you know' seem to operate sometimes as indicators of a break in the process of putting one's thoughts into words – a break which the listener is invited to fill in for himself from the shared stock of unformulated opinions: at other times they seem to appeal for confirmation of what follows. The question tag is an appeal for confirmation of what has just been said – confirmation, again, from the shared unspoken re- sources.

There are plenty of these expressions of sympathetic circularity in the mutually supportive speech of the previous examples – the five girls and the two. One might hazard a guess that such signals would feature in speech of that kind, but disappear when speakers engaged in argument. Bernstein has, however, suggested the con- trary: that when speakers of what he calls 'a restricted code' – a form of language which tends to be associated with the expression of shared attitudes and opinions rather than of individual differences – when such speakers are put in a situation requiring the elaboration of *differences*, they will tend to use the question tags all the more as a means of reducing 'sociological strain' – the anxiety, perhaps, they feel when they seem to be losing the support of group solidarity. It was interesting to note in the transcript that, as the argument warms up, 'like', 'sort of', 'I mean', 'you know', 'don't you?', and so on, tend to be replaced by the more emphatic form of appeal, 'right[?]' (which is sometimes a question – a demand for agreement, and sometimes a statement, a claim that there is agreement). If we divide the conversation into three equal parts, 'right[?]' occurs seven times in the first third, once in the second, and fourteen times in the last third, while the comparable figures for the other forms are thirty-six, thirty and sixteen.

I had a growing feeling as I studied the transcript that each of the speakers had some difficulty in believing the others could *seriously* hold an opinion different from his own. They appear to become puzzled, even aggrieved, as differences develop. At one point B makes a statement, C contradicts him and B says: 'No, no mucking about now, because, I mean . . .' and a little later C interrupts him with, 'No, come on . . .'. At all events it seems that each speaker supports his case by an appeal to something the group already accepts and possesses rather than to something they could now work out for themselves: that is to say, an appeal to *common sense* rather than an appeal to *reason*. The two are very different: common sense, it seems to me, is not a system of logically related, rationally held ideas; it is rather the accumulated representation of what one has 'got by with' in the past – an amalgam of factual knowledge, loosely empirical evidence, intuition, untested belief. If the appeal to what one takes to be a commonly held 'common sense' fails, and the appeal to reason cannot be made, the end is likely to be – as in this example – exasperation.

Argument seems to have a limited value for boys and

girls whose powers of talk are at the stages of those we have been considering. Even at a later stage, a good argument may put us on our mettle, but it is likely to be the thinking we do *after* it that is productive rather than the thinking we do in the heat of the dispute. The mutually supportive joint exploration, using a great deal of expressive language, is likely to be more productive *at the time*. I have suggested that A's contribution in the first example may illustrate the gestation of an idea: I suspect that a leap-frogging of listening and speaking may in fact be the characteristic feature of a joint exploration in talk and account for its value: each may give what he could not have given had it not been for the 'taking', and in turn what he gives may provide somebody else's starting point. If it works that way, talk would indeed be a co-operative effort yielding a communal harvest.

But clearly there must be the opportunity also to explore differences: it cannot be true that people can discuss usefully only matters on which they think alike. I wish to make two observations here. First, teachers need to find – somewhere in their larger context – an area of agreement within which their pupils can discuss differences. Failing that, they are space walking and that doesn't get them anywhere. It will follow that there must be some matters that cannot profitably be discussed between some people. Second, I want to refer to a form of discussion described by the American psychologist, Carl Rogers, and christened, therefore, 'Rogerian debate'. Roughly described, this is a process in which A tries on B's viewpoint and sees how the world looks from that angle – in particular that bit of the world about which differences of opinion have arisen. B is there to assist him and 'check his position'; when he is satisfied that his view has been adequately stated by A, he listens while A tries to say what he *finds in common* between his own and B's points of view.

A last word on the argument: we need to bear in mind the possibility that a satisfactory understanding may be reached, in ways that we do not yet understand, by the handling of implicit rather than explicit meanings. The difference between the two might be roughly similar to the difference between common sense and reason – though probably it would be more accurate to think of it as the two kinds of understanding which, in adulterated form, enter into 'common sense', and in purer form might be called reason on the one hand and intuition, imaginative wisdom – even poetic wisdom – on the other. Some of our group felt that the lack of explicit generalization and appeal to reason in the argument on education was not as crippling in its effects as I have represented it to be. Certainly, the joint exploration in expressive talk, and some informal modification of 'Rogerian debate', might prove valuable ways of handling implicit meanings; as well as a way of moving from the implicit towards the explicit, from expressive towards more referential uses of language.

The last transcript in this section differs from the others in many respects. The occasion is a science lesson with a first-year secondary school class, and the talk arises out of what the boys are doing and have been doing – heating copper in a flame. Again, though a good deal of talking went on among small groups of boys during the lesson, what is recorded consists in the main of what the teacher says. He talks first to small groups and later to the whole class. The tape comes from a film made by the Nuffield Science Project. (It was not possible to distinguish all the boys who speak, but A, B, C, etc., have been used to differentiate as far as possible the members of the group taking part at any one time.)

T Right, now. What do you think?
A It went . . .
B It's turned silver.
T Turned silver? Are you sure it's silver? Take it up to the front and have a look at it.
A It seems to have gone . . . red.
B . . . green.

T Yes, it looks as though it changes colour. What happens if you scrape it? Have a look.

B It's going . . . it . . .

A It goes pink . . .

T Do you think that's something that's formed on the outside, or what?

A . . . think it's . . . er . . . formed . . . er . . .

T What's happening then?

A A film's forming . . .

T A film? You think this is coming out . . . coming from inside the copper, do you?

A Yes.

B . . . combined with something in the air . . . to form the film.

T So you think something in the copper is . . . doing what?

B Is coming out . . . well, is combining with the air and forms that film.

T Yes. And what do *you* think?

C The same.

T You think the same? Well, *what* do you think – you tell me then . . . since you say you think the same.

C I think . . . there's something that's . . . er . . . combining with the air . . .

T Something combining with the air? Do you think you could think up an experiment to see whether the air is important in this?

A Yes . . . well . . . we could . . .

T Yes, well you think about it. I'm going to ask you all in a minute when you line up round the bench. All right?

A Right.

T O.K.

T Well, what about it then, A . . . ?

A Well, sir, it got . . . with something in the copper.

T Well where do you think it's coming from, this black powder?

A From the flame.

T From the flame? . . . something coming out of the flame? . . . See if you can think up something. . . . You think it's coming out of the flame. Do *you* think it's coming out of the flame?

B I think it's coming out of the copper, sir.

T You think it's coming out of the copper? Well, B . . . , see if you can think of things you could do . . . another experiment which would show which of you's correct. Anyway, think about it and I'm going to have you all up at the bench in a moment.

T [to the class gathered round the bench] Right, then. We've got three theories as to why the copper turns black when it's heated. We've got A's theory, which has six supporters, saying that it's something coming out of the air. We've got C's theory with four supporters saying that it's something coming out of the flame. We've got F's theory with eighteen supporters saying it's something coming out of the copper. Now obviously you can't *all* be right – and you've had some time to think over and work out an experiment to help verify your theory. O.K., then, A, what's your experiment?

A Well . . . suppose that's . . . air, I guess. . . . It would be a good idea . . . um . . . to . . . um . . . put . . . a piece of copper foil in a´ . . . in a . . . in a tube and . . . and put a cork in the end, and then take the air out of it with a vacuum pump. And then heat it. . . . If it turned black again it would prove our idea was wrong, but if . . . if . . . if it doesn't change, our . . . it would be right.

T Do you agree with that, B?

B Yes.

T Good. Now, what do the flame people think? [No answer] What do you think, C?

C Use another sort of foil and if that turned black then you'd know it was something in the flame. If it didn't, it wouldn't be something in the flame.

T Yes . . . any idea what particular foil?

C Lead foil?

T All right, we might try that. What about D, you got any ideas?

D No . . . the same one, sir – use aluminium.

T All right, well we'll try it. . . . But can anyone think of a way by which they could heat the copper so that the flame won't actually come in contact with it? What could you do to . . . E, any ideas from this group?

E Sir, you could . . . er . . . put copper foil in a test-tube over the flame . . . . then the flame won't be getting at the copper.

T Good – that's a good idea, isn't it? If you heat . . . if you heat the copper in something where the flame's not actually

touching. . . . Now, F, you're the spokesman for the copper
school. Now have you got any ideas on this?

F Well, you . . . you could repeat . . . um . . . A's experiment,
and if . . . um . . . if the copper turned black, that would
prove us right . . . um . . . but if it turned . . . if it stayed its
norm . . . it would prove A's group wrong as well.

It is a brief extract, but even so I believe it will speak
for itself to most teachers. 'Alternative possibilities' are
very much in the air – indeed certain alternative possibilities are what the lesson is about. And because they are
possible ways of explaining something pretty concrete and
specific, and because differences in the explanations
offered are going to be resolved in the end by further
concrete happenings in the laboratory, one may miss the
essential importance of the theoretical processes involved.

The first phase – the talk in small groups – is directly
concerned with possible explanations. Though the
teacher's questions are obviously a great help, he begins
on each occasion with a very open question: 'What do you
think?' and 'What about it then?' – saving his more
directive questions until he finds they are needed. No
doubt they will be needed less as time goes on – and more
will come from the boys in response to the open question:
indeed, in response finally to events themselves, regard-
less of the teacher. I was struck by his questions to C in
the first group: he seems to believe there is some virtue
in having C formulate for himself rather than take over B's
formulation. I believe also that the movement in words
from what might *describe* a particular event to a generalization that might *explain* that event is a journey that each must
be capable of taking for himself – *and that it is by means of
taking it in speech that we learn to take it in thought.*

The second phase is the mustering of the alternative
explanations and, from there, the devising of means to
verify them. The ideal in this – the most difficult part of
the task in hand – is that all the possible explanations of a
proposed experiment should be taken into account. Are
there some that would consider it a waste of time, there-

fore, that the teacher did not do this part of the job himself? He does in fact lay the burden on the boys' shoulders, and waits patiently while they talk their way through.

They are using in this extract – both teacher and pupils – a spare kind of language very different from that in most of the other examples. The reason for this lies in the nature of the activity of which the language forms a part. At the roots of scientific activity lie empirical operations: what is *done* in the chemical laboratory is of central importance and the language that serves such operations is closely related to processes – a language that may often be barely intelligible to someone who can't see what is being done. And when at the next stage (as in this example) words are used to explain the effects of what has been done or to devise plans for what *shall* be done, the generalizations must maintain firm connexions with the concrete data. True enough, wild speculation has its place in scientific activity, but the process of applying it, harnessing it, is one of re-shaping it in appropriately *specific* forms.

The spare look this language has may mislead us into thinking that it can easily be learnt. But the task is not that of learning a language; rather it is that of acquiring, *by the agency of the language*, the ability to perform these mental operations I have been talking about. *A child's language is the means*: in process of meeting new demands – and being helped to meet them – his language takes on new forms that correspond to the new powers as he achieves them. Expressive speech is one of the more accessible forms; the language of scientific hypotheses, spare though it may appear, comes later.

Acknowledgements

I should like to thank the following for help with transcripts and permission to quote from them; the British Broadcasting Corporation (page 82), Miss Margaret Frood, Mr John Kerry, Miss Nancy Martin, Mr Martin Richards, Mrs Pat Smyth, Miss Margaret Tucker, Unilever Ltd and the Nuffield Science Teaching Project (page 111), and Mrs Elizabeth Webster.

Part Three

Towards a Language Policy Across the Curriculum

A Discussion Document prepared and introduced by
Harold Rosen on behalf of the London Association
for the Teaching of English

Schools are language-saturated institutions. They are places where books are thumbed, summarized and 're-vised', notes are dictated, made, kept and learnt, essays are prepared, written and marked, examination questions are composed and the attendant judgements made. Teachers explain, lecture, question, exhort, reprimand and make jokes. Pupils listen, reply, make observations, call out, mutter, whisper and make jokes. Small knots gather round over books, lathes, easels and retorts, or over nothing in classrooms, labs, workshops, craftrooms, corridors and toilets to chatter, discuss, argue, quarrel, plan, plot, teach each other, using words to stroke or strike. There are foundation-stones, notice-boards, blackboards, pin-up boards, circulars, full of injunctions, warnings, records of triumphs, mottoes, cuttings, compositions and graffiti. As the school day unfolds law and lore become established, puzzled over or rejected.

In the penumbra of their attention most teachers have a kind of concern for language. It may be a desperate sense that their pupils' pitiful gropings for words and their botching together of a few tortured written sentences reduce their language to an absurd caricature. Or they may feel in a way which is rarely explicit that there are linguistic proprieties which belong with a subject for which they have a responsibility. More shadowy still is a sense that some kind of spoken contribution by pupils helps them to learn. How else can we explain that ubiquitous figure, the teacher as interrogator who emerges so strongly from Douglas Barnes' study? Finally, when they ask pupils to write they feel that much greater constraints must be imposed and they become more vigilant, more censorious and more censuring.

Boundaries must be clearly established and a chemistry student should write chemistry not history, autobiography or journalism. Douglas Barnes' study also shows us how in some teachers' language there are more delicate perceptions than those I have so baldly outlined. His study suggests that in the substratum of instructions, anxieties and prescriptions lies the promise of much more formulated notions of how language is working in their classrooms. In this attempt they are likely not only to make exciting discoveries about their own teaching but to discover something more general about language in education or how we use words to live. It is probably only through such a programme of patient self-education that so Utopian an undertaking as *A Language Policy Across the Curriculum* can become a working reality. I shall return to that theme later.

Douglas Barnes displays the teacher's strategies – his questions, explanations, coaxings – under a magnifying lens and that kind of exposure is bound to shed a somewhat ruthless light on any of us. Catch our most satisfying conversational moments on tape or in transcript and we wince. Yet somehow we must learn to wince, to take it, for the midwifery of new ideas insists on these pangs. What has been put under the lens is, of course, the teacher in his most institutionalized garb with, inevitably, language behaviour to match. There have been other ruthless studies of the teacher in this most formal posture which press us to ask whether the teacher must be both Chairman and Chief Speaker ('The Ringmaster' as Smith (1968) calls him). But we are interested in much more than the teacher's language. What is the *pattern* of interchange in many (most?) of those encapsulated curriculum units we call lessons? From his researches Flanders (1962) produced his simple arithmetic answer, his Rule of Two-Thirds, 'In the average classroom someone is talking for two-thirds of the time, two-thirds of the talk is teacher-talk, and two-thirds of the teacher-talk is direct-influence.' Some teachers on encountering this fact may well feel that

that is just how it should be; but to most it comes as something of a revelation which leads them to feel that they ought to make more space for pupil-talk and even that they should reduce their outflow of 'direct-influence'.

There is another study, little-known as yet, by Bellack *et al.* (1966), which investigated 'the patterned processes of verbal interaction that characterize classrooms in action' and tried to find out who spoke about what, how much, when, under what conditions and with what effect. This study too caught the teachers in their 'Ringmaster' instructional posture, teaching a course on 'International Economic Problems' to adolescents. Bellack's analysis followed up Wittgenstein's approach, 'the *speaking* of language is part of an activity, or a form of life' and various human activities are essentially linguistic in nature. From this he evolved his metaphor of 'language games'. Linguistic activities have definite functions to perform and can be likened to games because they have 'rules' for all 'players' and only certain moves are possible. Players have to learn the language rules and how various parts of the game are related. Teaching-learning is one of the games.

Bellack worked out the four basic moves of the game: the *structuring move*, which sets the context for subsequent behaviour ('Today we begin our unit on trade . . . etc.'); the *soliciting move*, which is intended to elicit a response, frequently verbal ('Now give me another reason' or 'Repeat that so that John can hear'); the *responding move*, which fulfils the expectation of the soliciting move, typically by an answer to a question ('Because they don't export very much'); the *reacting move*, which modifies or evaluates what has previously been said ('France. Right. And also Germany and Belgium' and 'Well, now that is not the question of course I asked'). These basic moves were then highly refined and the whole system much more elaborated. There is no space to outline it here but suffice to say that by using it the researchers were able to produce *The Rules of the Language Game of Teaching*, which turns

out to be a very lengthy code. As a complement to Barnes'
study I would make the following selection.

1. The teacher is the most active player in the game. He
makes most moves; he speaks most frequently; his
speeches are longest. The ratio of his speech to the speech
of all other players is three to one.

2. The major part of the game is played with substantive
meanings (i.e. the specific concepts of the lesson) specified
by the teacher's structuring.

3. Fact-stating and explaining are used much more
frequently than defining and interpreting. Opinions and
the justification of them are relatively rare.

4. The teacher is primarily a solicitor and the pupil a
respondent.

The picture which emerges from the work is one of enormous walls of constraint closing round the normal uses
of language or, to use the terms of the study, the language
games which are *not* played are just as significant as the
one which is. A different or modified code would be needed
to accommodate pupils talking to one another. Take this
anecdotal chain from a small group of ten-year-olds in a
primary class.

A   We used to have races in our house for getting dressed and
     um eating our breakfast quickly you see and we have er I
     er once I woke up in the middle of the night and the cur-
     tains were closed and I'd probably turn my light on so
     that in the morning you see Mum used to turn the light on
     so er I got out of bed went and got dressed and went
     downstairs to have my breakfast came up and woke Mum
     and I said to Mum 'What are you doing in bed Mum?'
     and she said 'What are you doing out of bed it's eleven
     o'clock'. I had to go back to bed with my clothes on.

J   Often when I wake up in the night I turn my light on and
     I can't make the effort to go and turn the landing light on
     I can't make the effort and I fall asleep with my light on
     and er once one Sunday morning I woke up . . . (in-
     audible) . . . What's the time? She said er, 'Eight o'clock'
     and I dashed out of bed and got ready as quick as I could

... I said 'Mum, I'll be late for swimming can I have a towel please?' She said 'It's Sunday.'

C   Oh my sisters never play chase with me I always go asking them but they're lazy they're all weaklings. I go outside and run around then Jean comes outside says 'Can I play?' I say 'No 'cos you know what for' and then she went inside and said 'Clare come out and play with me' and I went inside and said 'Can I play?' and they said 'No' and then yesterday Janine was after my ball and I threw it at her and it hit her wrist and then it went into Mrs Kidd's garden so I knocked on the door and er her daughter came and said 'What do you want?' and I said 'Can I have my ball back?' and she said 'Where's that?' and I said 'Behind the car. I chased after the ball' I said and she got hold of me and pulled me right across the grass and she went inside brushed herself down and she went inside and watched television.

J   When we were on holiday the week before last we were next door ... and made our own knocking code. I would just bash my head on the wall behind. I'd just pretend I'd bash my head on the wall and we had this knocking code you see. One it meant you know we had certain things 'Is it er is it alright for me to come in? Urgent you must come in now, see you in the morning.'

These sustained individual contributions might be contrasted with a sequence which would fit Bellack's system perfectly.

T   Well, anytime you taste sweat and tears, why does it seem to taste about the same level of saltiness? (pause) Blood. (pause) Well, think back to before we could think back. Before we were and were able to think.
P   Came from the sea
T   Came where?
Ps From the sea
T   What came from the sea?
P   Fish
T   All the ... what?
Ps Animals. Living things
T   All living things as far as we know. And everything happened in ... what?

P   In stages

T   In stages, yes. But everything happened, it happened in what?

Ps   In the sea. Evolution

T   Yes, evolution originally happened in the sea. O.K. So all life originated in what sort of environment, surroundings . . . ?

P   Water

T   What sort of water?

Ps   Salt, salty

T   Salt water, yes. In fact, all the processes that go on in our bodies must go on in water. In . . . what's the word? Things in water . . . dissolved in water . . . all the reactions?

P   Saturated

T   Well that's if you get too much

P   Solution

T   Yes, good. In solution. All the, you might say . . . chemical rearranging that goes on inside our bodies must take place in a salty solution, because when life as we understand it started, it started in what? In a salty solution. O.K.? And our blood is salty, and must be kept at the same level of saltiness, so we believe, as the sea was when we started, where our forbears started. O.K.? This is why the blood doesn't get any more or less salty. If we have got too little, when we sit down to dinner we somehow put a lot of salt on automatically, have you noticed that?

Walker (1969), in whose paper this transcript is quoted, says that focusing (his term) is a technique all teachers use, and that he has the impression that it occurs most often in the teaching of science. The features of focusing are the restriction of pupil participation to relevant, objective statements and the use of them to develop the idea on which the teacher intends to converge. He notes also the rejection of information and compression of knowledge. I feel he has selected a very recognizable example which probably we have all used some form of in our teaching, for better or worse, but want to ask how he construes the words 'relevant' and 'statement'. What is here considered relevant is the effort on the part of the pupils to guess almost the very form of words the teacher has in mind and, one hopes, move towards his meaning. Bellack's system would have that neatly docketed in a flash, but it could scarcely lay bare the delicate, slow, often apparently circular process by which we and our pupils move towards each other's meanings, nor does it seem designed to evolve the rules of that other language game, the Working Group Game, in which players, unmistakably in earnest, seek to get things done together by observing, thinking, investigating, planning and solving. The teacher's carefully composed structuring and soliciting moves, whatever their advantages, have the disadvantage of tightly circumscribing the responses and consequently of circumscribing the extent to which a pupil can formulate and represent in words what he is thinking.

The moment a conversation is started, whatever is said is a determining condition for what, in any reasonable expectation, may follow. What you say raises the threshold against most of the language of your companion and leaves open only a limited opening for a certain likely range of responses. . . . Neither linguists nor psychologists have begun the study of conversation: but it is here we shall find the key to a better understanding of what language really is and how it works (Firth, 1957).

If all conversation proceeds more or less on a single system in school classes then we have imposed the *same* limitation on all discourse, whereas in normal conversations the kind of limitation changes as our purposes change. Needless to say when we play the Language Game of Teaching we have to assume that there is a minimal concern to keep to the rules. An occasional rare pupil can spoil the game not by rowdyism but by refusal to play. Postman and Weingartner (1969) tell this story.

There is a sad little joke about a fifth-grade teacher in a ghetto school who asked a grim Negro boy during the course of a 'science' lesson, 'How many legs does a grasshopper have?' 'Oh, man,' he replied, 'I sure wish I had *your* problems!'

There are sharper criticisms yet to make of the game we have been looking at. They arise from the limitation of thinking resources called into play by the limited language resources. It is through the enormous variety of dialogue with others that we gather together the linguistic resources to dialogue in our heads; there is nowhere else to get them from. Restrict the nature and quality of that dialogue and ultimately you restrict thinking capacity. Out of the vast repertoire which language offers us very few items are left available to the pupil as a speaker, though the teacher himself uses a wider selection. This is what Mead was trying to teach as far back as 1900 (see the posthumous collection of Mead's work, published in 1934). He argued that an organized personality could emerge only through a capacity to take up the role of 'the other' and so to speak, carry it around with us. Language he maintained, put the intelligence of the individual at his own disposal.

But the individual that has this ability is a social individual. He does not develop it by himself and then enter into society on the basis of this capacity. He becomes such a self and gets such control by being a social individual and it is only in society that he can attain this sort of self which will make it possible for him to turn back on himself and indicate to himself the different things he can do.

The quality of our words in the head, inner speech, must be closely tied to our experience of talking with others which gives us resources for thinking and learning, for self-prompting and intellectual adventure. School could be a place where pupils enriched their resources, because it would be there that they encountered new verbal strategies and were inspired to more ambitious uses of language than those provided outside. James Britton shows in his section of this book some of the possibilities when the pupils take up the dialogue and begin to make the language moves for themselves, keeping the flow going as easily as they would at home or in a coffee-bar. He documents the group effort at understanding, the collective solution of a specific problem, joint exploration through expressive talk, the struggle to organize thoughts and feelings and, finally, the growth of explicitness. His transcripts show how teachers can begin to escape from the grip of the classroom interrogation and exposition and how the word 'discussion' can take on new meaning.

The reader will not have been slow to notice that throughout this book up to this point language has been more or less synonymous with speech, frequently, indeed, with something more modest which we prefer to call talk. I hope that as the argument has unfolded the reader will have appreciated that this viewpoint has been central to it, implicitly and explicitly. We are saying that it is as talkers, questioners, arguers, gossips, chatterboxes, that our pupils do much of their most important learning. Their everyday talking voices are the most subtle and versatile means they possess for making sense of what they do and for making sense of others, including their teachers. School should be a place in which we can hear the full sound of 'the conversation of mankind' (in Michael Oakeshott's phrase). How much more rewarding for the teacher to join this conversation as an adult voice and as an adult listener. Some children need to discover their voices, find their tongues, and some teachers need to rediscover theirs. When pupils are free to talk, teachers are free to observe and to understand what kind of learning is going on. For in the end, the teacher can only make sense of his pupils making sense. He can only work with their meanings.

As soon as students realize their lessons are about their meanings, then the entire psychological context of schools is different. Learning is no longer a contest between them and something outside of them, whether the problem be a poem, a historical conclusion, a scientific theory or anything else. There is, then, no need for the kinds of 'motivation' found in the conventional Trivia contest. There are few occasions for feelings of inadequacy, few threats to their sense of dignity, less reason to resist changing perceptions. In short, the meaning-maker metaphor puts the student at the centre of the learning process. It makes both possible and acceptable a plurality of meanings, for the environment does not exist only to impose standardized meanings but rather to help students improve their unique meaning-making capabilities. And this is the basis of the process of learning how to learn, how to deal with the otherwise 'meaningless', how to cope with change that requires new meanings to be made' (Postman and Weingartner, 1969).

Making new meanings. Exactly so, and we make them partly by talking our way towards them.

It may seem to some that under this dispensation schools would indeed become talking shops in which any sloppy, half-baked chatter was elevated to 'learning' and nothing ever got done. The versatility of language is such that exactly the opposite is true. A group of children go pond-dipping, or are working out the contour system from maps and models, or are investigating conditions in nineteenth-century factories, or are trying to design a tool to do a special job. Where does talk come in? Any or all of the following possibilities might be realized:

1. *Preparatory talk.* Some of this would be strictly practical planning – ways and means, some would be related to ideas, data, possibilities, some would be personal, expressive, anticipatory and some interpersonal (i.e. related to the social life of the group, its harmony and tensions).

2. *Talk on the job.* Observations, questions, speculations, formulations. Practical instructions, requests and decisions. Expressive language again, both personal and interpersonal, especially related to shared interest.

3. *Retrospective talk.* Recalling and savouring, ordering, concluding, debating, theorizing, suggesting new possibilities and further plans.

4. *Talking in the head.* The younger the children the more likely it will be that much of their activity will be accompanied by speech intended for no one else, i.e. giving themselves instructions or supplying a running commentary which is meaningful only in the context of the

activity (Luria's 'self-regulative' and 'synpraxic' speech). Older pupils will do much or all of this in their heads and, as I have already indicated, the quality and complexity of this speech will be highly dependent on the quality of their experience of speech with others.

If we examine the following entry from a mathematics teacher's log-book (it appears in the Crediton Mathematics Centre Report, n.d.) we can see some of these possibilities emerging. The reader is invited to try sorting out this talk using the above system or his own.

What is a Point?

This first discussion about a point came rather by surprise. The class had made some punched cards on which they had recorded certain details of their form, e.g. boys travelling by bus, by train, boys who stay to school lunch, etc. We had talked for some time about boys who came by train and also stayed to lunch, etc., and had used the cards to demonstrate this idea of intersection. When the intersection of 'boys who came by train' and 'boys who came by bus' was suggested the idea of an empty set came under discussion. It was during this that one boy likened it to a point!

What is a point? *It is a mere flick of the pen. . . . It's a dot . . . it could be round or square depending what shape pencil you had . . .*

How big is it? *As small as you can make it . . . smaller than that . . . you can't measure it . . .*

What happens if it is put under a microscope? *It will look bigger but will not be. . . . The measuring instrument would be bigger so it wouldn't help. . . . Really it's just an idea – something in the mind.*

The discussion moved on to 'position'. How many positions in this room? *Unbelievable. . . . One in every 10^6. . . . Can't count them. . . . The same as the number of points on a compass. . . . Depends on how many objects in the room. . . . Many more than quadrillions. . . . Don't be silly – everything is made so quadrillions would mean it took 10^6 years. . . . Depends on how big a molecule is. . . . Now he's bringing physics into it. . . . You would die before you finished. . . . No matter what answer you give it depends where* *you are seeing it from. If I stand in this corner there are millions over there and if I stand over there there are millions here. It doesn't matter where you stand they are still there.*

A few days later the class were asked to look at a white mark on the board for a few seconds. They were told to close their eyes and think hard about the point. Has anyone anything to say?

It's grown bigger . . .

Opening up into a lot of circles . . .

Mine's gone . . .

Getting bigger . . .

Looks like a cow . . .

Falling to pieces . . .

Two with a hole in the middle . . .

Two changing colour . . .

Growing legs . . .

Ball – like sun – bright shining orange . . .

Like flowers in a field . . .

Different colours all over the place . . .

Top half yellow, bottom half red – I've lost it now . . .

It keeps disappearing – comes back yellow – comes back red and green . . .

Cylinder shape opens out at bottom into oval . . .

Like looking at a strong light – mauve . . .

Two about ⅛" apart (R.H.S. yellow – L.H.S. green) going darker – turning into a ball about 3 times size . . .

Purple blob giving off green light . . .

Like a line 1" long – gone into circle ½" radius – green on yellow . . .

2 dots – big and little – big in foreground . . .

Breaking up – very bright background – spider's web – turning round . . .

Comments of this kind continued to come and more and more motion was being experienced – the children seemed deeply involved with their dot and were not at all interested in each others' comments. S's cow amused nobody. At times I asked a boy who had commented to keep me in touch with his point – this was done regularly and seemed to stimulate the 'dot' activity. There was no indication that any of the 'stories' were made up and I must admit to some fear at the excitement some children got from this – on one occasion W was talking about the blackish-yellow background eating up his dot. He became very excited as some sort of climax seemed imminent. I told him to open his eyes – he seemed relieved!

P suggested that children could not retain the image of a white dot on a black background with their eyes shut for a long period which prompted me to do the following short activity. I made a special effort, by continuous repetition, to make the children think of a white dot on a black board. I told them not to allow it to move, change colour or shape. They were then told to close their eyes and think hard about the situation and not to allow any change. A minute later (absolute silence during the minute) they opened their eyes and reported changes of colour, shape, etc. The changes were much more restricted but only three boys managed to keep the situation.

The following paragraph was produced after the weekend by a boy – I suspect he put himself back into the situation to write this.

'We drew a dot on the blackboard. We looked at it closely, then we shut our eyes. We tried to concentrate on the white dot. On my first go nothing interesting happened, but the opposite happened the second try. First of all there was just a black background but suddenly, a crooked line came in one half, blue the other half, red then a mustard colour enkalon carpet came. Then it faded away and it went to a bluey black background and lots of little white specks like stars. When that faded a beautiful light green and a dark blue came in. These colours were like fluorescent. Then a pineapple came in, it was like one of the tinned slices. When the lines came, a few more came in. They were like the red and blue. There was one a mustard and yellow colour and lots more others. Then we opened our eyes and we started shutting and opening our eyes. We did this because we weren't used to the light. Then we had our milk and talked about what happened.'

And talked about what happened. We can only guess at the details of that retrospective interchange round the milk bottles but in those outer ripples of classroom interest the talk was highly motivated and partly shaped by the variety of talk-with-activity which preceded it. They might have gone further with their mathematical speculation or more widely theorized about perception or simply rehearsed their experience. And the teacher's language glimpsed here shows him entering the talk in different ways but always by feeder roads not at the stop lights. At first glance it seems as though he restricts himself to the inevitable questioning procedure. But look at his questions and what follows from them. 'Has anyone anything to say?' is a pseudo-question and really an open invitation. We enter a different world of communication with 'I asked a boy who had commented to keep me in touch with his point'. In touch with the boy's 'unique meaning-making capabilities'.

A further question arises. I imagine that most teachers would find acceptable the debate about 'What is a point?' which opens the log-entry though some would raise an eyebrow at the fact that it 'came as rather a surprise' and wonder what kind of random syllabus is being followed. Nevertheless the debate seems recognizably mathematical, conceptual and cognitive, and could conceivably some time reach a pre-ordained conclusion. But what about all those performing dots? What irrelevance and wild self-indulgence! I imagine that the teacher himself might well answer that problems (the interesting ones) are best solved by viewing them in every possible way even the most unlikely, fantastic and idiosyncratic. In this way more possibilities are brought under review in novel ways and the problem may be seen to be a different one. Its multi-faceted surface is revolved and inspected from improbable angles. I would add that an essential part of this procedure is carried out by language just as we see the boys in the maths class shaping their possibilities in words. Indeed the whole exercise is centred on the word 'point', taken from the interlocking lexicon of mathematics. (A useful curriculum discussion might well begin with the question, 'To what extent can we say that the language of a subject *is* the subject?') The boys are learning to trust the tips of their tongues, that 'blurting out the first answer that comes into your head' has its uses and is not resorted to only by the idle and stupid.

But I would want to go further than this. Most of the understanding which schools attempt to inculcate in a highly organized way is embodied in language. In the varied fields of the curriculum these ways of saying and writing about things have been evolved by the most advanced scholars in those fields and have been followed by students and teachers. Sometimes they are followed blindly without an understanding of their rationale or their flexibility. What are finely adjusted systems of discourse become all too easily verbal rituals clung to like talismans in every field from literary criticism to physics. A common characteristic of these ways of saying is their impersonality; their cold neutrality is uttered by a disembodied voice marshalling abstractions and generalizations. They keep their distance and shift discourse from its specific context to a very general one, from the world of you and me and him to the world of 'one' and the passive voice, from this to that, from here to there. But this kind of public discourse is not a record of the thinking and talking which brought it into being, of how the individual talked himself into sense. That personal hinterland is populated with memories, images, attitudes, feelings and fancies which colour all our thinking. If we restrict the expression of new experiences to the most public, the most general, the most disembodied utterances we do so at our peril. Firstly, we price ourselves out of the market, for many children cannot talk this tongue. Secondly, as we have already suggested, we limit thinking. Thirdly, we repress a response which has value in its own right. We can go further yet. The acquisition of these forms of public discourse is a slow process. Personal expressive language is what springs easily to the lips of everyone, but mature specialized language can only be acquired by being differentiated out from other forms. The language in the textbook, on the blackboard and in the mouth of the teacher can be aped relatively easily, but this does not make it available for considered, appropriate, individual use.

I have perhaps made these points too cryptically. Let me expand on them a little. Let me take the last point first, namely the development of differentiated language. Everyone is aware, to a greater or lesser extent, of the differentiation of language; specialist writers on language with very varied viewpoints have given the question a great deal of attention. Laymen are all well aware that when they look at a poem written, for example, by a fourth former and at the same pupil's physics notebook they are looking at language functioning in different ways, just as they know that a newspaper's report of the day's proceedings in parliament is functionally different from that same newspaper's advice on how to kill lawn weeds or get rid of pimples. To be sure it is all English but we know that difference of function has, in ways which are often elusive, changed the language, so much so that after a sentence or two we know what kind of prose is likely to follow. Probably, if we go a stage further, we sense that the difference of function has meant a different stance on the part of the writer, a different psychological cast, if you like. He is about a different kind of business. We enter more difficult territory when we attempt to enumerate and categorize these differing functions into an orderly scheme or model. It is even more difficult if we attempt to do so in a way which is appropriate to the language of students of school age. Just such an attempt is being made by the Writing Research Unit at the University of London Institute of Education for the written language of secondary school pupils. Only the sketchiest indication can be given here of the Unit's model of function categories. The following extract from one of its documents will serve to illustrate the underlying ideas.

There are in our scheme three main categories:
Transactional

This is language to get things done: to inform people (telling them what they need or want to know or what we think they ought to know), to advise or persuade or instruct people. Thus it is used for example to record facts, exchange opinions, explain and explore ideas, construct theories; to transact business,

conduct campaigns, change public opinion. Where the trans-
action (whatever it is we want to do with language) demands
accurate and specific reference to what is known about reality,
this constitutes a demand for the use of language in the transactional category.

We shall need to subdivide this category in various ways, but
before going into this we shall describe the other two main
categories.

Expressive

Since 'expressive' covers a wider range of uses in speech than in
the written language, we shall consider the spoken uses first:

(a) Exclamations – expressions of fear, joy, pain, anger, surprise, etc. – made when there is no one there to hear them.

(b) More extended remarks we may make to ourselves to
express our feelings, put into words our immediate consciousness.

(c) Exclamations (as in (a) above) spoken in the presence of a
listener. (In these circumstances they will often be given and
received as in part an appeal for help, sympathy, some kind of
response. To interpret them fully the listener must know the
speaker and see the predicament, e.g. the proper response to the
boy who continually cried 'Wolf' would be to ignore it, unless
we could see the beast.)

(d) More extended speech addressed to a listener with whom
the speaker has a common understanding (shares experiences in
common: i.e. a listener whose context for the utterance will
largely coincide with the speaker's) and constituting an expression of the speaker's feelings, mood, opinions, immediate preoccupations; thus, what is said reveals as much about the personality and state of mind of the speaker as it does about the
events, etc., spoken about (e.g. Sometimes when I take my wife
out in the car, I drive and she talks – expressively).

(e) Interpersonal expressive. We have referred to a speaker
and a listener: to complete the account we must extend this (1)
to include more than two people and (2) to provide for the fact
that any listener may in turn become a speaker.

Applying now similar criteria to writing:

(a) The kind of writing that might be called 'thinking aloud
on paper'. Intended for the writer's own use, it might be inter-

preted by a reader who had shared much of the earlier thinking, but it could not be understood by one who was not 'in the context'.

(b) The kind of diary entry that attempts to record and explore the writer's feelings, mood, opinions, preoccupations of the moment.

(c) Personal letters written to friends or relations for the purpose of maintaining contact with them (as a substitute, so to speak, for being with them). Where the writer deals with his own affairs and preoccupations, the letter may read very like the diary entry (and a close relationship with the reader is claimed or assumed by regarding him as a 'second self'), but the writer may at other times more actively invoke a close relationship with his reader by (1) importing references to shared experiences in highly *implicit* terms and (2) implying strongly held shared opinions and values in the way he refers to people and events in general.

(d) Some writing of the following kinds may also, on balance, be said to have an expressive function:

1. Writing addressed to a limited public audience assumed to share much of the writer's context and many of his values and opinions and interests (e.g. topical newspaper commentary in a conversational manner, some editorials, 'interest' articles in specialist journals, gossip columns).

2. Writing, intended to be read by a public audience in which the writer chooses to approach his reader as though he were a personal friend, hence reveals much about himself by implication in the course of dealing with his topic (e.g. some autobiography).

From the examples of both speech and writing we can draw up the following *generalizations about the expressive function:*

(i) Expressive language is language close to the self. It has the functions of revealing the speaker, verbalizing his consciousness, displaying his close relation with a listener or reader.

(ii) Much is not made explicit in expressive language because the speaker (writer) relies upon the listener (reader) (a) interpreting what is said in the light of a common understanding (i.e. shared general context of the past) and (b) interpreting their immediate situation (what is happening around them) in a way similar to his own. It follows from (a) above that the meaning of an expressive utterance may vary in accordance with the situation. Compare the meaning of 'So, you're home 'at last' said by a wife in the small hours and by a mother at the airport.

(iii) Since expressive language submits itself to the free flow of ideas and feelings it is relatively unstructured.

Poetic

Poetic writing uses language as an art medium.

A piece of poetic writing is a verbal construct, an 'object' made out of language. The *words* themselves and *all they refer to* are selected to make an arrangement, a formal pattern.

(a) In all poetic writings the *phonic substance of language itself* is arranged (though the effect of the arrangement is generally more prominent, more sharply felt in a lyric than it is in a novel).

(b) The *writer's feelings* (about himself, about his topic, towards his reader, about the human condition) expressed naturally or casually in a piece of expressive writing, are in poetic writing ordered, arranged to create a pattern.

(c) Where there is a narrative, *the events* referred to make up or are part of a pattern.

(d) a pattern of *ideas*, a formal 'movement of thought', adds a characteristically poetic dimension to the writer's thinking.

These are not independent systems of arrangement, of course, but elements in a single significant design. Consonance and dissonance between formal elements bind the writing into a complete whole, a single construct (whether it be a sonnet or a novel, an epic or a curtain-raiser).

The phonetic, syntactic, lexical and semantic aspects of the utterance itself are the objects of attention, by the writer and the reader, *in a way that does not hold for non-poetic writing*. (We might roughly compare the two response processes with those of 'taking in' a painting and studying a map.)

The function of a piece of poetic writing is to *be an object that pleases or satisfies* the writer: and the reader's response is to share that satisfaction. In this sense, it constitutes language that exists *for its own sake* and not as a means of achieving something else.

(Perhaps it should be added that the nature and degree of the author's satisfaction must vary very much from one piece to another. The more complex the construct, probably, the greater the area of his experience that is lit by this satisfaction.)

The demand for *transactional* writing in school is ceaseless but *expressive* language with all its vitality and richness is the only possible soil from which it can grow. But many teachers who readily take delight in it feel that its proper place is in the English period when something called 'creative writing' or 'self-expression' is afoot. It is likely that right up to the last stages of secondary education the unfettered and honest expression by pupils of the meanings they have derived from their learning will be highly expressive and that their modes of expressing themselves will be very different from, and often better than, the strangled paraphrases of the average textbook writer. I imagine many teachers would still insist that it is their function to teach the proper language of a subject. There can be no quarrel with that but when? how? how much? And we need a further consideration of what that proper language is, when it is appropriate to use it and how pupils can be helped towards it. We can applaud every thoroughly absorbed feature which we notice in the pupil's work without feeling that we have also to censure unsuccessful efforts to use it or the absence of any effort at all. The time has come for all specialist teachers to discuss this subject and perhaps to codify their ways of using language. It would also be refreshing if specialist teaching included conscious attention to the language of their specialism. What, for example, is a 'proof', or a 'law' or a 'peasant'? Why do we not mention the broken test-tube or the colour of King Charles' hair? What are the problems in expressing in unilinear language non-unilinear processes?

Attending to the language of a subject is one way of attending to the subject. In this way the growth towards the appropriate transactional form can be through an understanding by the pupil of when and why he should modify his language from the expressive to the transactional on some occasions and can please himself on others. Finally, if we are right about expressive language, all teachers should be hospitable towards it. Most teachers are so already to some degree, particularly when they are talking to small groups and individuals. But when they call upon their pupils to write they are strongly affected by a kind of professional rigidity heightened by that conservatism which is inherent in the written word. Certainly many do not see the rewarding possibilities of the pupil's expressive view of their teaching and the insights it would give them into the responses they themselves have fostered – in expressive geology, for instance:

The Stone

It was formed, with the slates and shales, sandstones and clays, as a piece of hillside, long ago. Through the aeons, its limestone surface, mercilessly attacked by tropical storms and glacial nights, submerged in swamps and raised high on the heads of young mountains, has acquired the veins and wrinkles of human skin. Infinitely solid, and yet one can almost see through it to the heart of its being. It looks almost like a large, dull, irregular pearl, or a giant's tooth, with the grey-brown pits and streaks of sandstone bitten into it, like vast fillings. Underneath, where the brittle, eight sided pillar-nerves joined it to the gum, it has a crystalline glow when held to the light.
It is not a fiery rock, forged in the heart of a volcano, like rugged granite or tough basalt. It is a cool, serene piece of matter, born of water and retaining some of water's sheen.
– It is a piece of history, with a history of its own.
Stephen

I suggested that the expressive view had its own justification; this is particularly true when it moves towards the 'poetic' function. This is scarcely the place to justify the writing of poems and stories but it is the place to suggest that, since all experience is the potential raw material of expressive/poetic language, the deeper the feelings which are stirred by what is being taught the more likely it is that they will find their expression in poetic forms. It is unlikely, however, that a teacher will ever see such products unless his receptiveness to them is made apparent. A biology teacher could enjoy with a class this view of jellyfish not because it neatly illustrated a point but for its own sake and to share the writer's satisfaction with what he had made.

Jellyfish

I had learnt about it in Biology;
Yet now, as I toed it gently with my boot,
It seemed different,
Alien and strange.
I looked at it;
Pink and gleaming
It shone like a moonstone,
A quartz crystal,
Or an iridescent pearl.
Long tendrils splayed about
It had been abandoned by the sea,
Rejected by the tide,
To quietly melt and rot
On this lonely shingle beach.

Christopher

Even the pupil's view of boredom is to be preferred to simply witnessing it.

Geometry

Little arrows, following
each other round
a square.

Squares, within
squares, in different
colours.

Colours, distinguishing
lines, for which there are
many names.

Names, everlasting,
words, round which we wrap
our tongues.

Tongues, beginning
to talk, because we
are bored.

Yawns, like circles,
on our books, following
little arrows.

Bigger arrows, following
each other round
a square.

Leonie

It follows naturally that the variety of reading material the teacher puts before his class could be a happy complement to such an attitude. It should not seem far-fetched to picture a teacher of geography reading a passage from Alan Moorehead's *Cooper's Creek* or one of Henry Lawson's Australian stories, or a science teacher reading a science-fiction story or an extract from *Doctor Faustus*, or a history teacher from one of dozens of novels. Teachers in these fields could begin to compile for each other fascinating anthologies.

In discussing the functions of language I have inevitably included the written language. In spite of the fact that schools eat their way through mountains of blue-lined paper very little is confidently known about the *process* of writing as distinct from the product. What actually happens when a school pupil or a mature adult writes? What difference does it make to him if he is writing an entry in a diary which he locks away carefully rather than an account of the discussion which went on at the Congress of Vienna? Something is known, of course, and it should be taken into account when pupils are asked to carry out the thousand and one assignments which keep their heads down during the school day and often in the evening. Firstly, no matter how much a writer wants to write it is a hard and thorny business. We learn to talk almost effortlessly; almost everyone does everywhere and no special arrangements have to be made for us. But writing has to be taught in a more or less formal way. The writer is a lonely figure cut off from the stimulus and corrective of listeners. He must be a predictor of reactions and act on his predictions. He writes with one hand tied behind his back being robbed of gesture. He is robbed too of the tone of his voice and the aid of the clues the environment provides. He is condemned to monologue; there is no one to help out, to fill the silences, put words in his mouth or make encouraging noises. His reader will be tyrannical in a way which listeners cannot be, for he will be able to take his time in scanning the text and move to and fro in it. Listeners are usually waiting their turn anyway and some of their attention goes to their own imminent performance. The writer is thus under some compulsion to organize his utterance into a whole. He can no longer be the improviser he was as a speaker. He must become instead both more elaborate and more complete. He is unlikely to be given a second chance. No school pupil can be expected to do all this without help. He needs a reader more sympathetic than most. To ease the transition from speaker to writer he needs the help of reader-listeners, his classmates. There are practices which are still very common which do not help or help very little. I do not propose to list them. I want instead to suggest some questions which a school staff might jointly consider.

1. Does much of the written work consist of the pupil, in order to show what he knows, telling the teacher what he already knows so that he may judge whether the pupil knows it? Is it in fact a pseudo-communication?

2. Does the preparation for written work give the pupil the confidence that he has something of his own to say and can say it in his own words? Has the writing a helpful context?

3. Is the pupil confined to the repetition of facts? How does he know how to select the relevant ones and interconnect them?

4. How much freedom is there for comment, doubt, opinion, puzzlement?

5. Is the teacher the only audience? Or other pupils? Or others? Or the writer himself?

6. Does the pupil know what the writing is for ? To use for examination revision ? For future reference ? To clarify his ideas ? To publish them ?

7. Is the writing not so much composing as copying ? Verbatim ?

8. Does any writing ever arise from the pupils' suggestions ? Is the task identical for all pupils ? If it is, can they modify it ?

9. How is written work received. Is anything made of it or is it only marked ? Are there times for discussion of reformulations and re-structuring ? Does the writer believe anyone cares ? About what ?

Perhaps that is too much of a self-inflicted inquisition, though teachers almost anywhere would be happy to see a report of the joint attempt to supply answers.

Competent writers are readers not consumers of textbooks. They become competent talkers by attending to the flow of varied speech around them. Similarly, alone with his bitten pen the writer can go on scratching away largely because he knows how writers write and can select from the repertoire what suits his purposes. He will make mistakes; he will imitate one model too closely, fall in love with lurid phrases, concede too much to the reader or too little, but he will learn how to find his way about. Or will do so if he has access to a wide enough range of the written language so that he has some chance of noting differences of function and execution. If he meets the Factory Acts or the Thames Basin or the Balance of Payments only in one chapter in the class textbook, he is like a child who had learnt his mother tongue from a single speaker and a not very impressive one at that. There are written documents of all kinds other than books and a generous variety of books too. We have been shown the way very recently by the varied material published by the Humanities Curriculum Project and the Jackdaw Collections. Paperbacks are cheap enough for pupils and schools.

I have up to this point been trying to invite the reader to join me in a consideration of the ways in which language does and might enter school life. I have not been exhaustive, nor have I, I hope, been too ready with conclusions, remedies and marching orders. The matters I have discussed raise numerous questions, many of which are unresolved. But I have been trying to insist that we have not given sufficient attention to these questions and that curriculum discussions, curriculum reform itself can only be strengthened if it includes considerations of language and learning; that teachers who embark on observation, exploration and experiment concerned with the role of language in learning will make a valuable contribution to education, particularly if they also take a not uncritical look at the relevant literature.

My intention has also been to give the reader some sense of the thinking behind the document 'A Language Policy Across the Curriculum' produced by the London Association for the Teaching of English, for my own ideas and those of many others have been shaped by the hours and hours of work and talk which preceded and followed the appearance of that document. It is worth tracing the history of that document in various versions so that some sense of its potential can be appreciated.

In the L.A.T.E. we are all more or less specialist teachers of English and for many years we busied ourselves with our own fascinating specialist concerns with what did or would happen in the two hundred minutes per class of curriculum space allocated to us by the time-table. Increasingly, however, we found ourselves being pushed beyond the boundaries we had come to accept or perhaps helped to create. We found ourselves discussing the relationship between language and thought, how language represented experience, the functions of language in society, different kinds of language and how they were acquired, the difference between talking and writing, the nature of discussion and group dynamics. Inevitably we started to trespass in areas marked 'Keep Out', though some colleagues waved a welcome from the other side. There were others peering over fences, those engaged in integrated studies, group work, inquiry methods, environmental studies, social studies and innovations of all kinds. Some of them, though not many, were also concerned with questions of language. Soon we found ourselves talking about 'language in education', or 'language and learning', and finally about 'language across the curriculum'. We felt sure that language was a matter of concern for everybody, that if children were to make sense of their school experience, and in the process were to become confident users of language, then we needed to engage in a much closer scrutiny of the ways in which they encountered and used language throughout the school day. For this we needed all the help we could get from other subject teachers.

We started in May 1966, and we started – for reasons which have been made clear already in this book – we started with talk. At that time an emphasis on talk did not seem to be a radical idea: the word 'oracy' was already being used by educationalists alongside 'literacy' and 'numeracy'. We soon discovered, however, that the unanimity was a superficial one. *The Schools Council Examinations Bulletin No. 11*, for example, phrased the problem like this: '. . . they [the Steering Committee] recognize that the language of the coffee bar is not appropriate to school', and 'An idea of examiners deliberately coming down to the lowest teenage level was rejected, although the problem of contact was recognized' (p. 196).

By contrast, we were far from sure that we knew enough about the language of the coffee bar. We had certainly not settled what might be considered the appropriate language for school, though we knew quite well what was usually considered appropriate. It was largely for this reason that we began by looking closely at the language of children in various kinds of contexts and roles, both in the presence of adults and on their own. The questions we asked ourselves were:

What are the different kinds of talk used by children and
young people ?
What are their different functions ?
How does the size and nature of the group affect the
quality of the talk ?
How do different kinds of talk develop in the school years ?

We began making tapes of children talking in different
situations. We discovered that what we believed to be
reasonably skilled predictions – we are all experienced
teachers – were in many cases very wide of the mark. We
had imagined, for example, that a tape of children pre-
paring a meal would show them engaged in discussion,
and even argument and recrimination, about fair shares,
about who does what and the organization of clearing
away, about how much they should leave for the adults,
and so on. Instead of which the eating of food was accompanied by talk addressed to no one in particular which
simply named the foods, and the organization was carried
out quietly with only one or two subdued reminders –
more in the nature of spoken memoranda than exhorta-
tion. We discovered more too about the effect of the
presence of teachers – the way, for instance, the presence
of a respected and appreciated teacher created a sort of
psychological and social space in which less assertive
children could make a contribution and all members of
the group could engage in sustained talk. And most
important – since it is the kind of pupil activity that most
teachers by definition do not see much of – we learnt to
sketch in the outlines of the folklore of jokes, reminis-
cences and attitudes which held the group together when
there were no adults present. (Normal children spend a
great deal of their time laughing.) In this way we became
more certain that smaller groups were essential for certain
activities and that only small talking groups could address
themselves to problems in the way that so many children
on the tapes had done. Almost without noticing it, we
began to talk about language with scarcely a thought of

school subjects.

Our next move, of which this section of the book is in a sense a part, was not only to be concerned that the talk of schoolchildren should be given new importance and attention, but also to subject all uses of language in school subjects to closer scrutiny. We had found ourselves concluding that if we were committed to the development of children's language in school, then we needed to take a practical step towards making some impact on the way in which language was used throughout all the processes of school learning. This in turn meant that in any given school there needed to be a common approach to the uses of language. This task was in one sense straightforward and in another bristling with difficulties. It was straightforward because we aimed at drawing up a brief document – a 'manifesto' was the first grandiose term we used – which set out in unadorned terms what we thought ought to be done. It was difficult because we wanted the 'manifesto' to present a view that was relevant to teachers of subjects other than English.

This was, broadly speaking, the function of the L.A.T.E. Conference in May 1968. At that conference we attempted to broaden the terms of the inquiry, to see how far the outlines of our work and thought on talk could be extended to other kinds of language activity, and to draw up the first draft of a statement which could be circulated to schools for discussion and amendment. It is worth stressing, however, that very little detailed study of language in operation in the classroom is available to us, and in most cases we have had to rely on our combined wisdom and our critical assessment of our own practices. Douglas Barnes' paper which forms Part One of this book was one piece of detailed study; Nancy Martin and Alex McLeod of the Writing Research Unit of the University of London Institute of Education presented some preliminary findings as a result of a survey of one week's written work in five London schools. But for the most part it is uncharted territory.

Parallel to our earlier questions about talk, we went on to face questions of this kind:

How much writing and of what kind do pupils ordinarily do in and out of school (continuous and non-continuous, notes, exercises, etc.)?
What kinds of writing do teachers expect of pupils in different contexts, and why?
How does the nature of the writing task affect what the pupils write and how they write it?
What other influences (reading, conversation, etc.) might affect the way in which pupils write?
How do different kinds of writing develop in the school years?

But to return to the original document. It was produced from the heat of our discussions, produced by five working groups in half a morning, typed and duplicated in a lunch hour, finally sewn together and edited by a small committee. It appeared in the first edition of this book. When we produced it we were highly conscious of the fact that given more time, we could have refined it, that we could have consulted our colleagues more fully. But we were anxious to get started, for something to happen, to stir up wider participation, inquiry and collaboration. Probably this led us to phrase our policy in deliberately 'do this, do that' terms. We made too many assumptions and were too tempted to pithy slogans.

Many of those who encountered the document had no context to provide the thinking and experience behind it. We hope this book will go a long way towards remedying that, but it is clear to us that current ideas about the connexion between language and thought have not had wide dissemination. It would be one happy result of our work if it stimulated a growth of interest in such ideas. Other teachers felt that our tone was somewhat self-righteous or condescending. Perhaps we gave the impression to some teachers that most of what they are doing is wrong and that we know how to put it right. To this we can only plead that it is certainly not the case, though we did try to be fairly crisp and provocative in the hope that this would prove a better way of starting discussion. Others still expressed surprise that we should think our suggestions were in any way radical, while some have dismissed them as wildly impractical. About 'radicalness' we feel confident: our experience cannot be so far from the mark, and (as we have shown) we have a great deal of evidence to support us. The Discussion Document said at one point that 'the written language used by children must be their *own* expression of observation, ideas, conclusions', and we could fill warehouses with exercise books which do not even begin to meet that requirement. As for being impractical, we have been moved to undertake this work because like many others we have found that many of the old practices do not work. We are not unaware of the difficulties – examination syllabuses, the need to 'cover the ground', the wrong architecture and so on. But nothing we have suggested should make it more difficult for children to pass examinations, nor are any of our suggestions dependent on very desirable changes in school buildings.

A more intractable problem has been that some schools are not in the habit of organizing discussions about anything. They have neither the tradition nor the organization for formulating policies agreed on by the staff. It may turn out that we were wrong to assume that the best or the only way of starting was in the schools. Perhaps the powerful subject associations and the bodies which are undertaking curriculum experiments might be more effective initiators. However, we do not wish to be pessimistic. There are several schools which have taken up the idea of a 'language policy', and it may even be that schools not normally given to such procedures may have their first staff discussions on the issues we have presented. In so far as changes are needed, they are more likely to come about if teachers feel that they must remove obstacles which prevent them from teaching in the best possible way.

For all its faults the policy document has continued to produce encouraging results. In a number of schools, Teachers' Centres and colleges it has been a focus of discussion, and, more significantly, given rise to activities which we feel confident would not have occurred without it. Firstly, we have had critical comments and suggestions. What they reveal above all else is that teachers are beginning to examine for themselves the language of their pupils. Here is a report of one such examination. Its heading is worth quoting too, suggesting as it does a sustained interest in the questions raised by the document – 'Language Across the Curriculum III'.

M (Chairman) said he could see four problems in this area.

   (1) Note taking.

   (2) Essay questions – Kids can't always handle the language required.

   (3) Most material had to be given in wodges of words.

   (4) The experiences to be handled are remote.

H presented us with the following extract from a third-year Geography exam.

'Question: *Write all you can about the early explorers of America.* About 100 years ago a few men came to America they wanted to explor America. They wanted to be early explorers so they went all over the high and low mountains to explor then they went through the villages and over the lakes. They found out quite a bit about America they found out the names of all the states of America and kept it all down in a Record book so that he cooldent forget anything he found out the names of streets and roads and of course the names of all the mountains. the rested on mountains and on the land they did not have a lot of money But they had enough to keep them alive after they found out all they wanted to know they went back to there own country and so that is what the early explorers done.'

There was some discussion about this extract and some comparison with the extracts from the C.S.E. woodwork paper included in the last report. The fifth year boy had a better grasp of the facts than appeared in the Geography paper. Perhaps the Geography question could have been more precise. It would have helped had the third year writer been made to answer that question first orally in class.

J said that there were further problems here. If you ask a specific question then you get an answer which is just an enumeration of the facts. The children don't expand on the facts. It is very difficult to get exploratory communication.

M talked about a lesson he had had recently on the subject of lowering the voting age to eighteen. The class had not taken the problems far enough. Discussion could help here – kids could be pushed to question their own statements and see the implications.

P said this was a problem. The answers to a question tended to be all or nothing. J said we were asking for a very sophisticated level of activity when we asked for exploratory communication in History.

P gave an account of a piece of improvised drama with one of his classes. Columbus was asking Ferdinand for support for a voyage of exploration. The whole thing was over in ten seconds flat. There may have been a failure of imagination here but that was not the only failure.

M picked up one of the problems he had isolated at the start of the discussion. The experiences presented were remote, e.g. The vast majority of our kids have not seen a mountain. The same could be said to be true of many of the historical facts presented.

J felt that History should not be an isolated subject. The experience of History came mainly through the experience of words and this was an artificial extension of experience. D agreed. The pupils very often had not sufficient data to recreate the past in order to make this a real experience. Where we can give them sufficient data then they can project themselves into the situation. N added that concrete experience was needed. *Query by M.T. added while writing this up.*

Can English teachers help here? I've just emerged from reading *The Railway Navvies*, and *The Great Hunger* and *Famine and Insurrection* by Liam O'Flaherty with the feeling that there is a lot in each of these books I would like to read with English classes. Would it help if this were timed to reinforce work done in History classes? If so, could this be extended?

We have, we believe, stimulated a great upsurge of interest in the making of tapes, transcripts and the setting up of listening groups which are beginning to develop the skills of analysis. The L.A.T.E. has had functioning since its conference a Talk and Talkers Group which has accumulated an archive of tapes and transcripts of various lessons and situations which is ransacked regularly by those looking for discussion material. It has also kept in being a Language Across the Curriculum Group without whose activities this book could scarcely have been written, nor this section in particular. As far away as Evanston Township High School, Illinois, Miss Nancy Martin initiated discussions and a 'workshop' with teachers from all departments of the school, and the policy document was one of the main starting points.

Teachers of Science, Maths, Social Studies and Geography are becoming more and more involved not only in their own schools but also in their national organizations. The Association of Teachers of Mathematics has been the most prompt to join us in discussions and plan joint activities. Thus their members were able to read in their journal an article by one of our members, George Robertson, entitled 'Directions in English teaching', in which he says,

I think the 'modern' Maths and English teachers have much in common. They have implicit in their method a responsibility to know and understand the pupil in all aspects of his life which affect learning; that is, *all* aspects.

The commit themselves equally to re-examining from first principles the whole process of educational administration in its colossal effects on the crucial social interactions in learning of pupil and pupil, of pupil and teacher, and of teacher and teacher.

They imply various articles of faith and inspiration about the beauty and satisfaction of order, about the ability of men to respond as individuals with a desire for order, and about the nature of social order, which are quite evidently bones of contention in our society today . . . .

English and Maths teachers equally stand in the position of not only unlocking their culture for our pupils, but of modifying the ways in which they will perceive it (Robertson, 1969).

Close relations have been established with Science chiefly through the wholehearted participation from the outset of our venture of Mr Dick West who gave a science teacher's view of language at our conference. He has since then joined us frequently in planning and discussion and has put his views in print. In an article in *Forum* (1969) he writes:

Nuffield has emphasized the 'personal' nature of the pupils' record of work, and I think we must push this one stage further and break once and for all with the traditional sterility of scientific report writing with its emphasis on the impersonal. What the child does and sees is unique to him at the time it occurs and his report should be a unique communication. The experiences can then be generalized with a sense of involvement on the part of the participants. Not only is the generalization of events essential to scientific thinking, but the ability to generalize and relate our own experiences is essential to communication. Effective communication should lead to effective learning. It would appear that freedom for the child to express his experiences *in his own language* must come first. The language used may not be in itself scientific but it will be used in the context of a scientific experience. Out of this can grow the true language of science. Words used can become clothed with meaning and the child can move forward to effective classification of his experiences. The excitement of discovery need not be dampened by the problems of 'correct' verbalization.

Forum also found room in another issue (Spring, 1970) for an article by Peter Griffiths on language policy.

At one meeting a group of English teachers found themselves persuaded by a geography teacher to play a geographical game in which they had to be members of the Board of Directors of Iron Manufacturing Company. The report gives some idea of the discussion which followed the game.

Mr Hore pointed out that once the final decisions have been made the children are ready for the vital final stage, a comparison with the *real* situation (in this case it was a map of the present coal, iron and steel industries of England and Wales).

All the time they have been discussing the possible location of steel plants, they have been sneaking up to reality. Now they can discuss the unique situation in the light of the general tendencies they have established in their discussions.

Questions were asked about the amount of verbal information involved, and we looked at another more simple snakes and ladders type of game played on a stylized map using facts taught in advance. Writing produced during any game would range from private jotting to public and coherent statements. It was suggested that there might be different ways of looking at games. The English teacher would see the talk and discussion as being of first importance, but does a Geography teacher have to correct wrong assumptions? Mr Hore felt that he probably would, but that these could be pointed out when the real life situation is discussed and that on the whole there were no *right* answers. Answers as questions tend to be open-ended. It is the role of the teacher to compare the decision reached at the end of the game with the real-life situation.

As to the need to supply additional sources of information to which the children can refer while making their decisions, this depends largely on how far the age group using the game is capable of absorbing more information.

The question of patterns of speech and involvement was raised. Does conversation become complex and heated or does it tend to be at a low level? Mr Hore thought that it could be very lively and vigorous if the teacher was able to stand back and allow the children to really play out their roles. There was a possibility of the game becoming unscripted drama. This had happened when the postulated situation was a strike on a national newspaper and people had taken roles to resolve the strike.

We were hopeful that our bare suggestions would be filled out through the work of teacher groups and this is indeed beginning to happen. For example the peremptory dictum, 'Notes should never be dictated' which attracted some fire, has been constructively worked on by Miss Rosemary Leonard.

I refer to it not in order to demonstrate that agreement has been reached and the matter closed but because it shows how the debate can be carried a stage further. Only when our original document is amplified, modified and fortified with a thick batch of protocols will it really achieve its purpose.

Lastly, we are beginning to assemble a picture of how teachers see the language activities of their classrooms against the background of our suggested policy. There are two submissions from the dossier.

A Science Teacher: Secondary Modern

1. Encourage children to talk amongst themselves during experimental work. Constructive talk is always allowed and even a certain amount of 'social' chat, as long as children are predominantly concerned with the job in hand. Class discussion forms a large part of class activity. Usually I collect all kinds of opinions – both right and wrong – before attempting to arrive at a correct solution to a problem. I try to get children themselves to correct incorrect statements of others. I also encourage a very close teacher/pupil contact by chatting about almost anything.

2. In science, I always allow children to use their own familiar language in describing a situation. Scientific language is only suggested after they have been allowed free expression. They *never* copy work from a blackboard that may describe what or why or how something happens. Sometimes they will copy brief instructions, but where possible duplicated sheets are used. Spelling is corrected superficially only. I encourage children to describe accurately what they have observed.

3. School science journals are available in the lab.; charts, booklets and a science library are also present. Textbooks are mainly of the type giving experimental instructions, with a little 'padding'. Reference books are available in plenty and children are encouraged to use them.

4. Only C.S.E. candidates are encouraged to take notes. I find there is little enough timetable time for other classes and groups for them to be 'wasting' time other than doing and finding out.

Handicraft Teacher: Secondary Grammar

Comment Feel that language is important and must not be ignored in subjects such as woodwork and metalwork.

Talk Situations Boys managed to talk to me and discuss individual difficulties – these are then discussed with the group. Attempt to socialize the situation and discuss with boys other things in addition to problems connected with particular subject. Boys managed to express themselves in their own manner, no criticism of accent, dialect, etc. Students often take the 'role' of reader and suggest ways of changing the situation. Technical terms introduced when pupils are able to accept them.

Written Situations, Note-taking, etc. Note-taking used a great deal plus research work *but unfortunately* there is no co-operation with, or help from, other departments in the school. Examinations restrict experimentation in 'co-operative teaching'. Written work has to be highly technical in nature – when marking written work English is corrected as and when necessary. Again examination syllabi control a great deal, the attitudes towards what is 'handed in'.

Suggestions towards progress Closer liaison between departments and greater flexibility would assist in the development in Language Across the Curriculum. Grammar school teachers too often live in little 'boxes' with the examination results as ultimate goal.

I apologize in advance to the reader for this breathless Cook's tour of activities. I have had of necessity to keep the account brief but I have tried through quotation to give some flavour of the present state of the enterprise. I have not wanted to present an advertiser's picture of successful Treatment or Wonder Cure but rather to suggest to other teachers some of the varied ways in which the language policy might serve them. We were probably too optimistic in thinking that some schools would fairly rapidly produce a codified policy of their own and proceed to take steps to implement it. It is much more likely that the more modest and less dramatic activities of the kind I have reported on so briefly will constitute the preparatory phase, and they will have to become more widespread and influential. A first step towards this has been an expansion of activity from the London Association to the National Association for the Teaching of English. The Primary Committee has made a fine set of tapes of young children talking which will repay study wherever learning through talking is being discussed. Listen to this pair of infants (it is time we heard from them) examining a land-measuring tape.

Girl It's a tape measure . . .
Boy It only goes up to nine and starts at one again . . .
       Hey when you pull that out . . .
Girl How do you put it back in?
Boy Ah I know. . . . When you pull it out the think – the thing goes round and round – it's a handle . . .
Girl That goes up when you want it to if you turn it back . . .
Boy Oh yes, you turn it back.
       When you want it to go back *in* then when – if you want it to come out . . .
Girl Yes, you pull it out.
Boy When you turn that round that goes round.
Girl That goes round [Together]
Boy And when you turn it that way that goes round.
       [Laugh]
       [Repeat with different emphasis]
       That goes round, press that.
Girl What number does it go up to?
       Starts at one.
Boy Starts at one. . . . It comes what, it comes – first there's a red one, a red one.
       And then there's a black one, a black one.
Girl Well now that's one foot then it starts on another foot.
Boy Oh yea.
Girl And when it's a red one it's two feet . . . [Bang]
Girl Whoops . . .

Organizationally the debate and study will now be taken to national level; the 1971 Conference of L.A.T.E. will be devoted exclusively to Language Across the Curriculum and its various commissions will consider talk and discussion, the book and the textbook, writing and kinds of writing, language and thought, and the role of the English teacher.

We have undoubtedly come a long way since we sat in small groups (less than two years since the time of writing these words) and tried to spell out what was meant to be a dramatic challenge. Since then we have rendered obsolete our own document, which is just as it should be. We have tried again with mark 2 which follows this final section of this book. Some readers will have copies of mark 1. They might derive some interest from comparing the two.

We have perhaps without realizing it been following the promptings of that great pioneer of language studies, J. R. Firth, who as long ago as 1935 was urging us to give our full attention to what he called 'the biographical study of speech'.

We are born into a vast potential cultural heritage, but we can only hope to succeed to a very small part of the total heritage and then only in stages. There would appear to be a need to emphasize that for each stage of childhood and youth, for each type of child, there are a relevant environment and relevant forms of language. There is a vast field of research here in what may be called the biographical study of speech. There is material for all the branches of linguistics in the study of all the various components of meaning in this linguistic life-history of the young person as an active member of his age-group as well as a pupil, in his seven ages of childhood and youth.

There is plenty for us to do. To that end we should talk to one another.

References

Bellack, A. A., *et al.* (1966), *The Language of the Classroom*, Teachers College Press, Columbia University,

Crediton Mathematics Centre (n.d.), *Logbook*, Report No. 3.

Firth, J. R. (1957), 'The technique of semantics', in *Papers in Linguistics, 1934–1951*, Oxford University Press.

Flanders, N. A. (1962), 'Using interaction analysis in the in-service training of teachers', *Journal of Experimental Education*, vol. 30, no. 4, pp. 313–16.

Griffiths, P. (1970), 'Language policy', *Forum*, vol. 12, no. 2.

Mead, G. H. (1934), *Mind, Self and Society*, University of Chicago Press.

Postman, N., and Weingartner, C. (1969), *Teaching as a Subversive Activity*, Delacorte Press,

Robertson, G. (1969), 'Directions in English teaching', *Association of Teachers of Mathematics Supplement*, no. 13, November.

Schools Council, *Examination Bulletin*, no. 11.

Smith, L. M., and Geoffrey, W. (1968), *The Complexities of an Urban Classroom*, Holt, Rinehart & Winston.

Walker, R. (1969), 'A sociological language for the description of the stream of classroom behaviour', Centre for Science Education, Chelsea College of Science and Technology (unpublished paper).

West, R. (1969), 'Reflections on curriculum reform', *Forum*, vol. 12, no. 1.

Acknowledgements

My thanks for help of various kinds are due to: my colleagues in the Writing Research Unit of the University of London Institute of Education; Stephen Harvey for 'The Stone'; Christopher Naylor for 'Jellyfish'; Leonie Richards for 'Geometry'; members of the staff of Walworth Secondary School for the minutes of their discussions on 'Language Policy Across the Curriculum III'; Peter Hore for the report of the geographical game; and the Primary School Sub-Committee of N.A.T.E. for the tape produced by the 'Children Talking' Group.

A Language Policy Across the Curriculum

Language and the Teacher

Language permeates school life. Boys and girls in their attempts to master the school curriculum and in the process of growing up have to call upon their language resources. Moreover they are expected to increase these resources by making the language encountered in their school learning a living part of their thinking and communicating. We take the view that we have chosen a most promising moment to put before *all teachers* a document which will open discussion on the educational implications of these obvious facts. We think it is a promising moment because teachers of all subjects and in all kinds of schools are becoming aware that language is inextricably bound up with all the learning that goes on in school. They are becoming acquainted with the research on the relationship between language and thought, with theories on the acquisition of language and with work on the nature of language itself, for these ideas are finding their way into the most important educational debates of our day. Innovations in the curriculum and the discussions which surround them have helped to focus attention on language. We believe that many teachers are now prepared to go far beyond the older view that language was someone else's business, or, perhaps, that they were the guardians of linguistic proprieties. They are now prepared to consider what needs to be done to improve our procedures in schools in such a way that language becomes a facilitating force in learning rather than a barrier bristling with formidable difficulties.

For all the dissemination of new ideas relatively little has been done to work out in detail just what needs to be modified or changed in our day-to-day practices in order to achieve solid advances. We still have ahead of us that crucial and demanding phase of realizing in classroom practice the theories which seem so promising. Therefore we want to move discussion to this stage.

We would like to see more teachers of all kinds and of all specialisms talking together about language, their pupils' and their own in all its variety. We would like them to join us in studying how changing situations change the productivity and potentiality of talk. We would like them to join us in considering the differences between speech and writing and what it means to the young writer to compose in words his own observations, conclusions and attitudes. We would like them to observe with us the effects of giving scope to the full expression of the personal view in all new learning. We would like them to consider critically with us what we offer pupils to read in school books and to decide how pupils can best make sense of the printed word. We want to go beyond wringing our hands at the low level of literacy, at shrinking from contemporary speech manners, at frustration in the face of inarticulacy and reticence. We want instead to evolve a realistic programme that could be implemented by any school which was convinced that a change was necessary and possible.

Language and the Pupil

In children's encounters with the curriculum there is a confrontation between their comfortably acquired mother-tongue and the varieties of language which have grown up around institutionalized areas of learning. In many of these areas special demands are made on their thinking – they are expected to reason, speculate, plan, consider theories, make their own generalizations and hypotheses. These are in many respects language activities, that is, language is the means by which they are carried out, the means, therefore, by which children do much of their learning. The effort to formulate in the pupil's own words the appearance of something, or to draw conclusions from an experiment, or to express the significance of an historical document is an essential part of the learning process, for he will be using language to give meaning to his experience. But there are formal mature ways of expressing these things which have arisen in a different context, are designed to meet different expectations and are directed at more or less public audiences. The school pupil is remote from such a situation and its attendant language needs. His healthiest need is to make sense in his own terms of what he is learning. It will take many years of development before his situation begins to approach that of the scientist, historian, technologist, etc. This stage is likely to be reached towards the end of his secondary schooling.

Mature language is highly differentiated, modified to meet many differing and complex functions. Some of these functions require from the mature adult that he inhibit all those features of language which are the expression of personal and inter-personal feeling in the interests of dispassionate objectivity and undistracted communication. Since these are very sophisticated achievements we cannot expect to find them in school pupils. If such writing is to develop at all it must grow out of the confident use of personal expressive language and the thoughtful, conscious consideration of the new language the teacher has to offer.

Talking

The speaking voice precedes the writing pen and the reading eye in the life-history of every normal child. Given the opportunity and a favouring environment he can use it to do more things than he can do with the written word. Through improvised talk he can shape his ideas, modify them by listening to others, question, plan, express doubt, difficulty and confusion, experiment with new language and feel free to be tentative and incomplete.

It is through talk that he comes nearer to others and with them establishes a social unit in which learning can occur and in which he can shape for public use his private and personal view. Thus we think that school learning should be so organized that pupils may use to the full their language repertoire and also add to it. From our discussion and exchanges of experience we would make these suggestions.

1. Many school activities should be carried out by small groups which can use their talk to move towards understanding by means which are not present in the normal teacher-directed classroom.

2. Though much of this talk may seem uneconomic, tentative and inexplicit, it is often the only way in which genuine exploration can occur. Teachers can frequently help forward discussion at the crucial moment, but probably we need less intervention and more patience.

3. We need to find ways of helping pupils without putting words in their mouths. We could perhaps be less concerned to elicit from them verbatim repetitions of time-honoured formulations than to ensure that pupils engage in a struggle to formulate for themselves their present understanding. Discussion is an essential part of that process.

4. Teachers should encourage pupils to consider the language of the subject in ways which are appropriate to their development. Time spent in considering why reports, observations, theories, etc., are expressed in one way rather than another should be an essential part of intellectual development. We all need to learn more about the language of our subjects.

5. Room should be found for speculation and fantasy.

6. As teachers we might free ourselves much more from situations which confine our own language to the most formal exposition and most limiting kinds of questions. Talk with small groups and individuals gives the teacher greater linguistic scope and make it possible for

him to influence the pupils' language more profoundly
We need to experiment more with questioning so that it
leads to fuller and more adventurous responses.

We acknowledge that more talk by pupils creates its own
problems and that not all talk is productive. We need to
identify these problems and find ways of overcoming
them.

Writing

The written language has the advantages of permanence,
completeness and elaboration. It gives the writer the time
and scope to examine his own language and fashion it
more precisely to his purposes. Yet young writers are
frequently at a loss when confronted with a typical school
assignment or they are reduced to summaries and paraphrases from textbooks and notes. Some of their difficulties are an inevitable part of the transition from the
spontaneous spoken word to the new and complex conventions of the written word. Other difficulties arise from
special features of the school situation. Much they are
asked to write is broadly speaking informative; yet no
genuine informative act is taking place, i.e. no one is being
informed. The tasks frequently seem to lack a clear function, nor do they seem to leave room for the expression of
the writer's own ideas and his way of seeing things. All too
rarely in school writing assignments is the writer expressing something he wants to say to others.

It is probably in the written work of pupils that the most
stereotyped and uniform language is to be found. We do
not believe that most teachers *prefer* it to be like this. How
could it be changed?

1. By written work arising as a logical need from the
learning in hand – the need to record, to report, to propose
solutions, to weigh possibilities, to sort out ideas, etc. The
ideal to aim at is the genuine need to communicate something to somebody. An exchange in talk beforehand is
likely to help pupils discover this communicative need.

2. By greater tolerance for the pupil's own expression of his observations, ideas and conclusions, and the positive encouragement of very varied responses including personal imaginative ones.

3. By discussing with pupils the formalities and conventions of particular kinds of documents (e.g. laboratory records, notes, etc.) and allowing them to devise their own.

4. By avoiding stereotyped conventions irrespective of the function of the writing and by encouraging appropriateness of response. The impersonality of certain kinds of prose is appropriate only for certain purposes.

5. By encouraging self-initiated work and providing generous choices or at least the possibility of modifying the set task.

6. By attempting to develop a genuine sense of audience not only through a genuine message from pupil to teacher but also by widening the audience to other pupils in the class and school and people outside the school.

7. By breaking the bonds of the school 'exercise' designed to be completed in a standard homework stint or school period and written in a standard exercise book. More sustained efforts can be made with books, pamphlets, displays, etc., and may be the result of a successful collaboration.

It follows from these suggestions that written work asks for the teacher's attention and interest more than (perhaps, instead of) his marks. If prior and exclusive attention is given to spelling, punctuation and correctness (in its narrowest sense) then all too easily the writer feels that the message itself and his effort to communicate it are of less importance. If his writing is made more public then he is more likely to develop the incentive to become his own editor and to set himself higher standards of presentation.

Many hours are spent by pupils *copying* notes but many pupils never learn how to *make* them. This would not only be for many an investment in their educational future but would be for all part of the process of learning. They would be engaged in abstracting and verbalizing the essence of what they had learnt. Moreover, note-making could be their living experience of how writing needs to change as its function changes, for notes will be different in kind as the writer's purposes change. The co-operative composition of notes under the teacher's guidance; a set of notes made by pupils for each other's use; the study of extracts from the note-books of scientists and writers; these could all help to build up a notion of the varied criteria for the selection and presentation of material. The dictation or copying of notes then may seem to be a quick and efficient method for accurate learning but in the long run actually omits a vital process in teaching.

Reading

The books made readily accessible by teachers not only provide an inexhaustible supply of material by means of which pupils can teach themselves and supplement what has been taught, they also represent the chief means by which they can learn the varied adult forms of discourse and when they should be used. The standard textbook supplied to every member of a class can scarcely fulfil such ambitious requirements even if it is well-written. Frequently it is not. Many textbooks seem to be addressed to the teacher rather than the pupil and their language shows little awareness of the kinds of linguistic difficulty confronting the pupils they purport to address.

The excellent work already done by teachers and librarians has pointed the way to the following suggestions.

1. Pupils should have access to all types of reading material relevant to the topic they are studying, reference books, newspapers, periodicals, cuttings, documents, stories, biographies.

2. They should have the opportunity to observe the varied emphases, commitments, attitudes and presentation of different writers.

3. Textbooks should not be treated as sacred sources of

irrefutable data but rather as one of many sources of handy reference. For the study of some topics the school textbook may well be dispensed with.

4. For children who have difficulty with reading, material should be taped and the tape made available with the text. Pupils might make some of these tapes.

5. There should be time for reading in class not only for specific assignments but also for reading of a more exploratory kind.

6. The teacher should read aloud material which is compelling and provocative.

The Teacher

The teacher's role in schools is changing and much of what we have proposed is in line with this change. The more teachers work *alongside* their pupils the more likely it is that our suggestions will make sense. The more they foster the initiative of their pupils the more likely it is that their pupils will develop a confidence in their own use of language. The less they attempt to verbalize ideas for their pupils the less stereotyped will their pupils' language be.

How Could the Policy be Implemented?

1. Teachers in schools, teachers' centres, etc., should pool their observations of language in use in school (including, of course, their own). They should examine in detail specific problems, e.g. teachers' and pupils' questions, the language of textbooks. Teachers with different specialisms should compare their problems, e.g. Is note-making in history different from note-making in chemistry?

2. Subject associations should devote conference time and meetings to language problems, e.g. The metaphors of biology.

3. Wherever possible teachers should attempt to make themselves familiar with relevant recent studies and

researches on the nature of language, how it works and how it is acquired.

4. Small-scale investigations should be made by teachers to furnish documents, tape and videotape for their discussion, e.g. the use of language on a field-trip including the preparation and follow-up.

5. Arising from discussion and investigation it should be possible for some schools to put into operation a language policy which would act as a guide to *all* their teachers. Such a policy would, of course, be developed and modified in the light of the experience gathered from its formulation and application and would, therefore, be shaped to meet the needs of specific schools.

As a step towards implementing the last suggestion we put forward this document. It is not, we would emphasize, a blue-print but a starting-point. We would be disappointed if it were taken over lock, stock and barrel.